OUT OF THE DEPTHS

OUT
OF
THE DEPTHS

THE PSALMS SPEAK FOR US TODAY

Revised and Expanded Edition

By
BERNHARD W. ANDERSON

THE WESTMINSTER PRESS
Philadelphia

Published by The Westminster Press®
Philadelphia, Pennsylvania

PRINTED IN THE UNITED STATES OF AMERICA

9 8 7 6

ACKNOWLEDGMENTS

Darton, Longman and Todd Limited and Doubleday & Company, Inc., for Scripture verses from *The Jerusalem Bible*, published and copyright 1966, 1967 and 1968 by Darton, Longman and Todd Limited and Doubleday & Company, Inc.

National Council of Churches, Division of Christian Education, for Scripture verses from the Revised Standard Version of the Bible, copyrighted 1946, 1952, © 1971, 1973.

Random House, Inc., for lines from "For the Time Being" and from "New Year Letter," from *W. H. Auden: Collected Poems*, by W. H. Auden. Copyright © by Edward Mendelson, William Meredith and Monroe K. Spears, executors of the Estate of W. H. Auden.

Library of Congress Cataloging in Publication Data

Anderson, Bernhard W.
Out of the depths.

Bibliography: p.
Includes index.
1. Bible. O.T. Psalms—Text-books. I. Title.
BS1430.5.A53 1983   223'.206   83-19801
ISBN 0-664-24504-8 (pbk.)

In memory of my mother,
Grace Word Anderson

Psalm 22:10

CONTENTS

PREFACE

It is reported that Athanasius, an outstanding Christian leader of the fourth century, declared that the Psalms have a unique place in the Bible because most of Scripture speaks to us, while the Psalms speak *for* us (see the *Service Book*, p. 45; United Church of Canada, 1969). There is much truth in this observation. Much of the Bible, in the conviction of the community of faith, is the medium of God's speaking: "the word of God in human words," to cite a familiar expression. But the psalms of the Old Testament are different. Here, for the most part, we find people addressing God in response to God's overture, in the moods and modes of lament in times of distress, of thanksgiving in times of liberation, and in hymnic praise in times of rejoicing in the goodness and wonder of God's creation and providence. In this sense, the Psalms may speak "for" us, by expressing the whole gamut of human response to God's grace and judgment and thereby teaching us how to pray.

This book, which in its first edition was used experimentally as a study guide, is now being released in a modified and expanded version as a brief introduction to the Psalms. As the reader will notice, it is written primarily for the Christian community of faith, though this purpose is not intended as a limitation but as an attempt to understand the psalms in the appropriate setting: the setting of worship. The book may be used in classes or study groups, or it could serve as a *vade mecum* (Latin, meaning "go with me"), a medieval name for something carried about by a person as a guide or reference.

This study finds a way through the 150 psalms of the Psalter by means of the so-called form-critical method, that is, the study of psalms according to genres that can be classified on the basis of their literary form and setting in worship. The reader will want to refer to the appendixes at the back of the book where the classification is conveniently given.

Since this is not intended as another book *about* the Psalms but rather a guide *into* the Psalms, it is extremely important that you read the psalms themselves carefully, following the study plan as it unfolds chapter by chapter. In each chapter, groups of psalms are taken up according to their type and setting in worship, and major theological issues arising out of these psalms are discussed. If you cannot read all the psalms in these categories, read at least those recommended (marked with an asterisk in the lists given in the various chapters).

Assuming that you cannot read a psalm in the original language (Hebrew), it is important for you in your study to consult more than one modern translation, such as:

Revised Standard Version (RSV)
Jerusalem Bible (JB)
New American Bible (NAB)
New English Bible (NEB)
New International Version (NIV)

When a translation from one of these is used, the abbreviation of the version is given: e.g., Psalm 22:10 (RSV). In many cases, however, I have given my own translation. In these instances, nothing follows the citation of chapter and verse.

Each chapter, besides treating psalms that belong to a specific genre, will lift up some important theological question with which the community of faith wrestles as it rereads the psalms in the contemporary world. These questions include: the knowledge of God, the enemies that threaten us, the power of death, the name (identity) of God, the advent of God's Kingdom, and the problem of suffering.

Since the interpretation of Scripture takes place within a community, not only a community of worship but a community of scholarship, I should like to thank the many persons who have influenced me, directly or indirectly, in this work. Also my thanks go to my graduate student Suzanne Boorer from Australia, who has helped me in the final stages of editing the manuscript. Finally, I extend my thanks to the publisher, The Westminster Press, for the execution of this project and especially to the religious book editor, Dr. Paul Meacham, and the editorial staff.

It is hoped that the study of the psalms will lead to a deeper understanding of the meaning of worship and that these prayers will speak for us "out of the depths"—to cite the opening words of Psalm 130—of our human experience.

B.W.A.

Princeton Theological Seminary

1
THEOLOGY
IN SONG

In our troubled and traumatic times there are many people who can identify with the experience of the ancient Israelites after the exodus from Egypt when, according to the story, the short route into the Promised Land was cut off and "God led the people around by the way of the wilderness" (Ex. 13:18). Those who belong to "a pilgrim people" come to realize that the goal of their journey through history is not reached by the easy highway; instead, they must take the roundabout way, the detour into "the wasteland" (T. S. Eliot) which poets and artists have portrayed. In a Chorus from W. H. Auden's "For the Time Being: A Christmas Oratorio," we hear:

> The Pilgrim Way has led to the Abyss.
> Was it to meet such grinning evidence
> We left our richly odoured ignorance?
> Was the triumphant answer to be this?
> The Pilgrim Way has led to the Abyss.[1]

Yet in this present time of "wandering in the wilderness" something remarkable has happened. Participants in the community of faith have learned to praise God anew, not just in times of God's presence but in those times when, to use an expression that frequently occurs in the psalms, "The face of God" is hidden (Ps. 10:11; 13:1; 30:7; etc.). Just as early Christians sang songs of praise while in prison (Acts 16:25), or in other difficult situations, so in our turbulent period of history, when the foundations are shaking and the world seems to be on the verge of chaos, people in church and synagogue join their voices in singing "psalms and hymns and spiritual songs" (Eph. 5:19).

This was the experience of one German pastor—who later became a professor at the University of Heidelberg—in the time of World War II. While in a German prison camp, Claus Westermann had with him a copy of Luther's translation of the New Testament and the Psalms, and so he turned to the study of the Psalms according to Luther's free version. Out of his life and thought he wrote about what these songs meant to many people in times of trial:

> Whenever one in his enforced separation praised God in song or speech, or silence, he was conscious of himself not as an individual, but as a member of the congregation. When in hunger and cold, between interrogations, or as one sentenced to death, he was privileged to praise God, he knew that in all his ways he was borne up by the church's praise of God.[2]

Others too have testified that the psalms have enabled them to speak to God "out of the depths" (to cite the opening words of Ps. 130) in company with the invisible believing and worshiping community.

This was eminently true in the case of Dietrich Bonhoeffer, the martyred Christian whose writings have profoundly influenced contemporary theology. One of his last writings before he was executed for conspiracy in a plot against Hitler was *The Prayer Book of the Bible: An Introduction to the Psalms* (1940). He begins this tiny book with the observation that the Psalter is a prayer book, that is, the words that worshiping people address to God. How, then, can these prayers to God be, at the same time, God's word to the people? Bonhoeffer answers this question by saying that these are the prayers God gives us to pray in the name of Jesus Christ, who has brought every human sorrow and joy, every frustration and aspiration before God. If we prayed out of the poverty of our heart, we might pray for only what we want to pray; but God wants our prayer to be much fuller, encompassing not only our own needs but the life of the whole community of God's people. So just as the Lord's Prayer was given in answer to the request, "Lord, teach us to pray" (Luke 11:1), so the book of Psalms is teaching about how we are to come before God in the proper way. It is therefore quite appropriate, in this view, for the New Testament and the Psalms to be bound together, for the Psalter is "the prayer of the church of Jesus Christ" and "belongs to the Lord's Prayer."[3]

THE PSALTER AS A CHRISTIAN HYMNBOOK

The bracketing together of the New Testament and the Psalms, as in the case of the Lutheran edition, just mentioned, points to the important place of the psalms in Christian worship.

From the very first, Christians treasured "the book of Psalms," or "the Psalter," very highly. As a matter of fact, the title "the book of Psalms" comes from the New Testament (Luke 20:42; Acts 1:20). In the Hebrew Bible the title is *tehillim*, which means "songs of praise." The early Christian community, however, read the Old Testament in the Greek version (Septuagint), where the prevailing title was *psalmoi*, referring to songs sung to the accompaniment of stringed instruments. One codex of the Greek Old Testament used the title *psalterion*, a term that referred basically to a zither-like instrument and secondarily to songs with stringed accompaniment; hence the alternate title "Psalter." The early followers of Jesus of Nazareth expressed their faith in the singing of "a new song," yet this "new speech from the depths," as Amos Wilder points out, drew deeply upon fountains that sprang up within worship.[4] The early church was profoundly influenced by synagogue worship in which psalms were read as scripture, recited as prayers, or sung as hymns.

Down through the centuries the psalms have enjoyed an indispensable place in the liturgical practice of the church. Today in Roman Catholic and Eastern Orthodox churches the entire Psalter is recited. This is true likewise in Anglican churches.

[The former monastic practice of reciting the psalms once each week has been modified. Today Roman Catholic monasteries might celebrate the Psalter in a two-week cycle; and in the Liturgy of Hours worshipers recite the Psalter on a four-week cycle, with appropriate variations. The entire Psalter is included in the Anglican Book of Common Prayer for liturgical use; the present practice is to recite the Psalms in a seven-week cycle, with appropriate variations or omissions.]

In churches in the Protestant tradition the profound influence of the Psalter is evident in the responsive reading of selected psalms or in the singing of hymns influenced by psalms, such as "All People That on Earth Do Dwell" ("Old Hundredth," Ps. 100) and "A Mighty Fortress Is Our God" (the great Reformation hymn, Ps. 46). Indeed, when one considers the enriching and invigorating influence that the psalms have exerted upon preaching, worship, and devotional life, it is no exaggeration for Christoph Barth to say that "the renewal and reunion of the Church, for which we are hoping, cannot come about without the powerful assistance of the Psalms—without the support of their incomparable words, and above all of their imperishable message."[5]

The early Christian church did not appropriate the Psalter of Israel because it lacked the inspiration for composing new hymns with a distinctive Christian accent. Students of the New Testament are becoming increasingly aware of hymnic fragments and other liturgical materials embedded in early Christian literature. For instance, in the magnificent portrayal of the humility of the Christ "who, though he was in the form of God, did not count equality with God a thing to be grasped, but emptied himself, taking the form of a servant" (Phil. 2:6-11), Paul made use of an early Christian song that was familiar to his readers. Fragments of Christian hymnody are contained in the "new song" of Rev. 7:9-14, which Handel transposed into the triumphal music of *Messiah* ("Worthy is the Lamb who was slain . . ."). And the Gospel of Luke includes two complete Christian psalms: the Magnificat of Mary (Luke 1:46-55) and the Benedictus of Zechariah (Luke 1:68-79). The Benedictus begins this way:

> *Blessed be the Lord God of Israel,*
> *for he has visited and redeemed his people,*
> *and has raised up a horn of salvation for us*
> *in the house of his servant David,*
> *as he spoke by the mouth of his holy prophets*
> *from of old,*
> *that we should be saved from our enemies,*
> *and from the hand of all who hate us;*
> *to perform the mercy promised to our fathers,*
> *and to remember his holy covenant.*
> *—Luke 1:68-72 (RSV)*

Here the language echoes that of the psalms, including the theme of deliverance from enemies (Ps. 23:5); but this is *a new song*, pitched in the brilliant key of the good news that in Jesus Christ, God "has visited and redeemed his people."

What has happened in the New Testament is that the Christian community has appropriated the whole body of Jewish scriptures—in Christian terms known as "the Old Testament"—and in so doing has "baptized the Psalter into Christ."[6] Along with the prophecy of Isaiah, the

Psalter is one of the two Old Testament books most frequently drawn upon in the New Testament (see Appendix C). Early Christians, who regularly used the book of Psalms in worship, wanted to say that these songs bear witness to Jesus Christ. Thus the royal psalm, Psalm 2, with its divine declaration "Thou art my Son," was understood to refer to *the* Anointed One (Messiah), Jesus Christ; and Psalm 22, a song of lament beginning with a poignant cry of dereliction, "My God, why hast thou forsaken me?" was taken to be a portrayal of Christ's passion.

In saying that these and other psalms refer to Jesus Christ, the early Christian community was associating itself with the People of Israel, whom God had formed and consecrated. Christians confessed then, as they do now, that the Old Testament is indeed part of "the story of our Life," as H. Richard Niebuhr once put it,[7] a story of God's involvement in the life story of Israel that leads to and is illumined by God's visiting the people in the event of Jesus Christ: his life, death, and resurrection. In this perspective it may be said that the entire Psalter—not just those psalms which are interpreted "christologically" in the New Testament—is illumined by the Christ event. This conviction is beautifully illustrated in Luke's post-resurrection story of the walk to Emmaus (Luke 24, especially vs. 27, 44-47).

It is important to keep in mind, however, that the native setting of the psalms was the community of ancient Israel and, in particular, Israel's service of worship in the Jerusalem Temple. There the tones of Israel's praises were heard as the people remembered and celebrated the sacred story. Christians ought to be in tune with the psalmists and let the rich sonorities of Israel's worship be heard, even though they hear the psalms in a different liturgical setting. Perhaps this matter may be clarified by a figure of speech that musicians will readily appreciate.

The same notes may have a different tone quality when the sounding board is changed, for instance, from violin to cello, or from harpsichord to piano. Even so, to Christian ears the notes of the psalms have a fuller and deeper resonance when played against the sounding board of the Christian liturgy which celebrates God's saving activity and presence through Jesus Christ.[8] Accordingly, it is customary in Christian worship services to conclude the responsive reading or the chanting of a psalm with the ancient Christian hymn, the Gloria Patri.

PSALMS OF THE PILGRIM PEOPLE

Our discussion of the role of the early Christian community in composing and interpreting psalms leads to a very important point. The psalms of the Bible are not individualistic poems such as a modern person might compose to express personal thoughts and feelings. Rather, the psalms show that the individual finds his or her identity and vocation in the community that God has created. Within that community of faith one has access to God in worship; and within that community one participates in a great historical pilgrimage. As we are reminded in the documents of Vatican II dealing with the church, the Bible presents the story of "God's Pilgrim People."

It should not be surprising, then, to discover that the songs of this pilgrim people are not confined to the Psalter but are found in connection with the whole unfolding story of the Bible—not only in the New Testament, as we have noticed, but throughout the Old Testament. More and more we are coming to learn that many of the materials in the Old Testament, such as the story of creation in Genesis 1:1–2:3, were shaped by liturgical usage, perhaps in connection with one of the great Temple festivals. In addition, numerous psalms are scattered throughout the Old Testament. As a preface to our concentrated study of the book of Psalms, it would be helpful to glance over some of these Old Testament psalms. The list includes:

1. The Song of the Sea (Ex. 15:1-18), composed to celebrate Yahweh's (RSV "the Lord's") deliverance of the people Israel from Egyptian bondage. (Based on the Song of Miriam, Ex. 15:20-21.)

2. The Song of Moses (Deut. 32:1-43), a song that contrasts God's faithfulness with Israel's unfaithfulness.

3. The Song of Deborah (Judg. 5:1-31), a victory song composed to celebrate Yahweh's coming to the rescue of the embattled "people of Yahweh" (end of v. 11).

4. The Song of Hannah (I Sam. 2:1-10), a psalm of thanksgiving inserted into the story about Samuel at Shiloh.

5. David's Song of Deliverance (II Sam. 22:2-51), a psalm of thanksgiving, preserved also as Psalm 18.

6. A song of thanksgiving (Isa. 12:4-6) used to conclude the first section of The Book of Isaiah.

7. King Hezekiah's song (Isa. 38:9-20), a psalm of thanksgiving for use when presenting a thank offering in the Temple.

8. The prayer of Habakkuk (Hab. 3:2-19), a hymn praising Yahweh for divine victory on behalf of the people Israel.

9. Jonah's prayer from the belly of a fish (Jonah 2:2-9), actually a psalm of thanksgiving.

10. Hymns embedded in the prophecy of Second Isaiah (e.g., Isa. 42:10-12; 52:9-10) which summon the earth to sing "a new song."

11. In The Book of Job there are both hymns (e.g., Job 5:8-16; 9:4-10; 12:7-10; 12:13-25) and laments (e.g., Job 3:3-12, 13-19, 20-26; 7:1-10; 7:12-21; 9:25-31; 10:1-22).

12. Psalms of lament are also found in The Book of Jeremiah (e.g., Jer. 15:15-18; 17:14-18; 18:19-23) and in Lamentations, especially chs. 3 and 5.

If we were to consider literature belonging to the expanded form of the Old Testament (i.e., including the books often called the Apocrypha), other psalms could be added to the list. For instance, in Ecclesiasticus (otherwise known as The Wisdom of Jesus the Son of Sirach) we find the thanksgiving of Sirach (51:1-12) and superb hymns of praise (39:14b-35; 42:15–43:33). Also in the popular story called Tobit, from around the second century B.C., there is a magnificent hymn of praise (Tobit 13). And though we cannot go into all the relevant literature outside the scope of the Hebrew Bible, special mention should also be made of the beautiful songs found among the Dead Sea Scrolls, apparently composed by members of the Qumran monastery for use in their worship services. In accordance with liturgical styles in vogue in the synagogue, these hymns fall into two main categories: thanksgivings ("I give thee thanks, O Lord . . .") and blessings ("Blessed art thou, O Lord . . .").[9]

Even this cursory review shows that the psalms preserved in the Psalter represent only a small selection of the many psalms that once were composed and sung in Israel. For the Bible as a whole is not only the story of God's dealings with a particular people but also this people's response in thanksgiving and adoration, in lament and petition along the way of its pilgrimage through history. The sounds of Israel's praises are heard, to one degree or another, in practically every book of the Bible, from Genesis to the Revelation to John. It is in the Psalter, however, that the praises of God's people resound clearly as nowhere else.

THE PSALMS IN THE HISTORY OF WORSHIP

On first glancing through the Psalter we discover that the 150 psalms are arranged into five parts, or "books." The structure of this songbook is as follows:

Book I   Psalms 1-41
           Concluding doxology: Ps. 41:13
Book II   Psalms 42-72
           Concluding doxology: Ps. 72:18-19
Book III Psalms 73-89
           Concluding doxology: Ps. 89:52
Book IV   Psalms 90-106
           Concluding doxology: Ps. 106:48
Book V   Psalms 107-150
           Concluding doxology for entire
               Psalter: Ps. 150

Notice that each of the first four books concludes with a brief doxology that is not a literary part of the psalm with which it is associated. Psalm 150 not only fittingly concludes the last book but rounds off the entire Psalter with a doxology.

Just as the Psalter appropriately ends with an invocation to praise, so it suitably begins by striking the keynotes of Israel's faith. It is not accidental that the Psalter in its present form opens with two key psalms: Psalm 1, which extols the virtue of meditating on the Law (Torah); and Psalm 2, which was regarded in the late Old Testament period as referring to the Messiah (literally, "the Anointed One"). These two themes—the revelation of God's will in the Torah and the hope for the coming of the Messiah to inaugurate God's kingdom—constituted the two cardinal beliefs of the Jewish people at the time the Psalter was given its final form.

This fivefold arrangement of the Psalter was made relatively late in the Old Testament period and was undoubtedly patterned after the Torah (Pentateuch) which was divided into five books (Genesis through Deuteronomy). In its present form the Psalter comes from the period of the Second Temple—the Temple of Zerubbabel, which was rebuilt in 520-515 B.C. (the time of the prophets Haggai and Zechariah) and stood until it was superseded by the Temple of King Herod (begun about 20 B.C.), the stones of which may still be seen in the famous Wailing Wall of Jerusalem. Sometimes the Psalter is spoken of as "the hymnbook of the Second Temple." This is proper insofar as the Psalter was given its final shape and was used in Temple services during this period. Yet this was also the period when the synagogue was emerging as the focal point of prayer and interpretation of scripture. Therefore the Psalter may be called the prayer book of the synagogue with equal justification, especially since it opens with a psalm that reflects the piety based on the study of the Torah.

As a matter of historical fact, the rise of the synagogue was a major factor in keeping alive the faith and tradition of Israel in a time when Jewish colonies were springing up outside Palestine. Alexandria in Egypt came to be one of the major centers of the Jewish "dispersion" in the postexilic period. About 250 B.C. the Alexandrian Jews began to translate their sacred scriptures into the vernacular—which for them was the ordinary Greek of the Hellenistic world. This Greek version of the Old Testament (known as the Septuagint) contains a Psalter that differs in several interesting respects from the Hebrew tradition followed by the Protestant Reformers. For one thing, the Greek Old Testament—like the scriptures of the Dead Sea community of Qumran—contains an extra psalm (Psalm 151)[10] which is attributed to David. The Greek Bible also differs somewhat in the determination of where a particular psalm begins and ends; for instance, what is regarded as one psalm in the Greek Bible may appear as two in the Hebrew Bible (e.g., Ps. 9-10; 114-115).

The early Christian community, being Hellenistic in complexion, read its Old Testament in Greek. Accordingly, the structure of the Psalter in the Greek Bible has influenced Christian usage, as may be seen from translations used in Roman Catholic and Eastern Orthodox communions in the past. In this study, however, we shall follow the numbering of the Revised Standard Version—a translation that has been accorded the status of "the Common Bible" by Protestant, Roman Catholic, and Eastern Orthodox representatives. Even this numbering will have to be questioned at points, for some psalms reckoned as two in the Hebrew Bible (and hence in the Common Bible) actually constitute one literary unit (e.g., Ps. 42-43); and vice versa, a psalm that is considered as one may actually consist of two literary units (e.g., Ps. 27). In other words, the numerical determination of the psalms does not always coincide with the literary units, as we shall see. (See the listing in Appendix B.)

One further detail deserves to be mentioned at this point. Generally speaking, two words for deity are used in the Psalms: one is the word Elohim (God) and the other is the personal name YHWH, the so-called Tetragrammaton (four consonants) which, in the judgment of scholars, was once spelled Yahweh. During the biblical period, the personal name came to be regarded as so sacred that it was withdrawn from ordinary usage and the substitute

Adonai (Lord) was pronounced. The Jewish reverence for the Name has influenced most modern translations which, following ancient synagogue practice, substitute Adonai, rendered as "the Lord" in English, "der Herr" in German, "El Señor" in Spanish, and so on. In this study, however, we shall retain the name Yahweh, as is done in the Jerusalem Bible and in some Roman Catholic services of worship.

> [*The Book of Common Prayer* (1977), in its preface to the Psalter, has an explanatory note on this subject, pointing out that the synagogue practice is to be followed except for two passages where "the context requires that the Divine Name be spelled out." These passages are Psalm 68:4 and Psalm 83:18.[11]
>
> [It should be noted, too, that the Septuagint (the Greek translation of the Hebrew Bible), made in Alexandria, Egypt, just before the rise of Christianity, also used the substitute "Lord" (Greek, *kurios*). Since the early Christian community read the scriptures of Israel in Greek, this synagogue custom is also found in New Testament quotations from the Old Testament.]

Let us return to our consideration of the Psalter as a whole. A closer look at the fivefold structure of the Hebrew Psalter reveals that this symmetrical organization was superimposed upon previously circulating collections of psalms, just as a modern hymnbook is based upon previous editions of hymns of worship. Evidence of this is found in the editorial notice at the end of Psalm 72: "The prayers of David, the son of Jesse, are ended" (Ps. 72:20). This postscript is rather surprising when one discovers that psalms of David, according to their headings, are found later on: Psalms 108-110 and Psalms 138-145. This can only mean that at one stage in the history of the formation of the Psalter a Davidic collection ended at this point.

When we look at the psalms up to this point (Ps. 3-72; minus Ps. 1 and 2 which are introductory to the whole Psalter), we find that there are actually two groups of psalms which, by their headings, are ascribed to David: namely, Psalms 3-41* and Psalms 51-72.

[*Two of the psalms in the first Davidic collection, Psalms 10 and 33, are not explicitly ascribed to David. Psalm 10, however, is actually the second half of an alphabetical psalm, i.e., one in which every second verse begins with a successive letter of the Hebrew alphabet. The first half of the alphabetical sequence is Psalm 9 (ascribed to David), and thus Psalms 9 and 10 should be considered one psalm, as in the Septuagint. The other psalm in question, Psalm 33, is ascribed to David in the Septuagint.]

In between these two Davidic collections we find a group of psalms ascribed to Korah (Ps. 42-49); and just after the second Davidic collection we find another group ascribed to Asaph (Ps. 73-83). We gather from the book of Chronicles (written about 300 B.C.) that Korah and Asaph were leaders of musical guilds during the period of the Second Temple (see, e.g., II Chron. 20:19). It seems likely, then, that the original nucleus of the Psalter was the Davidic collection found in Psalms 3-41. In the course of time this collection was supplemented with other Davidic collections (especially Ps. 51-72), and with various collections composed and used by the choirs of the Second Temple (Ps. 42-49; 73-83; 84-88). Eventually the collections now found in Psalms 90-150 were added. In this last section of the Psalter we find, for instance, a group of psalms that celebrate Yahweh's kingship over the earth (Ps. 93-99, except Ps. 94). Another group is characterized by the exclamation "Praise Yahweh," which in Hebrew is *hallelujah* (Ps. 111-118; 146-150). And still another group bears the superscription "Song of Ascents" (Ps. 120-134), an expression that probably means "a pilgrimage song," that is, a song used when pilgrims ascended to Jerusalem to worship at the Temple. Psalm 122, for instance, expresses the pilgrims' joy on having arrived at their destination.

I rejoiced when they said to me,
    "Let us go to the temple of Yahweh!"
Our feet were standing
    within your portals, O Jerusalem!
                    —Psalm 122:1-2

In summary, we find embedded within the present edition of the Psalter the following collections:

(6)

1. An original Davidic collection (Ps. 3-41)

ELOHISTIC
PSALTER

2. Psalms of the Korah musical guild (Ps. 42-49)
3. A second Davidic collection (Ps. 51-72)
4. Psalms of the Asaph musical guild (Ps. 73-83 + Ps. 50)
5. Additional psalms of the Korah guild (Ps. 84-88, except Ps. 86)
6. Various other collections (Ps. 90-150), including:
    a. Psalms of Yahweh's kingship (Ps. 93-99, except 94)
    b. Songs of Praise (Ps. 103-107)
    c. Psalms of pilgrimage (Ps. 120-134)
    d. A third Davidic collection (Ps. 138-145)
    e. Hallelujah psalms (Ps. 111-118; 146-150)

The collections shown with a brace in the above outline (Nos. 2, 3, 4)—the so-called Elohistic Psalter—at one time circulated as a separate hymnbook. This is evident only from the text of the original Hebrew Bible, in which all these psalms show a decided preference to use the general name God (Elohim) instead of the special divine name Yahweh (RSV "the LORD"). Some statistician has computed that in this Elohistic Psalter (Ps. 42-83) the divine name Elohim appears 200 times and Yahweh only 43, whereas in the rest of the Psalter, Yahweh appears 642 times and Elohim only 29. The best explanation for this striking phenomenon is that the collection once existed independently before it was included in the final framework of the Psalter. This would explain why two psalms appear in almost identical form: Psalm 14, which uses the name Yahweh, and Psalm 53, which uses Elohim.

It is appropriate, then, to speak of the Psalter as "the hymnbook of the Second Temple" if we keep in mind that, like a modern church hymnal, it is a relatively late arrangement based on previous collections and including hymns of many ages. This is true, for instance, of *The Methodist Hymnal*. It includes hymns from the Patristic period ("O Guide to Every Child," by Clement of Alexandria), from the Middle Ages ("Creator of the Stars of Night," anonymous), from the Reformation (Luther's "A Mighty Fortress Is Our God"), from the period of the Enlightenment (Addison's "The Spacious Firmament"), from the great Wesleyan revival ("O for a Thousand Tongues to Sing"), to say nothing of modern hymns that reflect the pietism of the nineteenth century or the theological renaissance of the mid-twentieth century. Similarly, the Psalter, though it received its final form three or four centuries before Christ, reflects a long history of worship, reaching back at least to the time of David and, in some instances, including forms of worship used by Israel in the early period of the settlement in the Land of Canaan. It may cover as much as a thousand years of the history of worship.

THE AUTHORSHIP OF THE PSALMS

In another respect, however, the comparison of the Psalter with a modern hymnbook does not hold. Most of the songs in our hymnbooks are assigned to definite authors, whose dates are usually given in connection with the tune. Relatively few modern hymns are anonymous; indeed, numerous books have been written about the authors of our great hymns. In the Psalter, however, the situation is just the opposite. The authors of the psalms are unknown, and practically nothing can be learned from the psalms about the time or circumstance of their composition.

This statement may sound surprising in view of the traditional belief that the book of Psalms contains the very words of David. Since the beginning of the Christian era, and indeed right to the nineteenth century, David has been regarded as the author of the Psalter. This view is reflected, for instance, in Mark 12:35-37 which reports Jesus' dispute with the scribes over the lineage and identity of the Messiah. The argument assumed that "David himself, inspired by the Holy Spirit," wrote Psalm 2, although in the Psalter this psalm, unlike many others, does not have a heading that attributes it to David. Jesus' argument, however, was *ad hominem*, that is, it was addressed to the prejudice of the scribes and was not intended to be a critical discussion of the authorship of the psalm. When it is assumed elsewhere in the New Testament that the Psalter is Davidic (e.g., Acts 4:25-26; Rom. 4:6-8), the writers merely adopted the contemporary way of referring to the hymnbook of Israel. In the same manner people of the time identified the Torah (Pentateuch) with Moses or the Wisdom Literature with Solomon.

Even on critical grounds, however, the association of David with the Psalter is substantially valid. There was an ancient tradition, to which the prophet Amos appealed in the eight century B.C. (Amos 6:5), that David was skillful with the lyre. It was this skill that brought him into the court of King Saul, according to a well-known story (I Sam. 16:14-23). Moreover, David gave great impetus to Israel's worship by bringing the Ark of the Covenant to Jerusalem (II Sam. 6) and by laying plans for the building of the Jerusalem Temple (II Sam. 7). Further, there must be considerable truth in the view expressed in the relatively late Chronicler's History that David sponsored the composition of psalms and was active in organizing the music and liturgy of Israel's worship (I Chron. 13-29). In the light of all this it may be assumed that embedded in the Psalter are poems or poetic fragments actually composed by David or by those in his court. An example is Psalm 24, especially its concluding portion (vs. 7-10) with its address to the gates of Jerusalem to lift up their heads so that the "King of glory" may enter—a ritual that clearly recalls David's bringing the Ark into his new capital.

Not all the psalms, however, are attributed to David. The Psalter contains psalms attributed to the choir leader Asaph (12 psalms), to the Sons of Korah (11), to Moses (1—Ps. 90), to Solomon (2—Ps. 72 and 127), to Heman (1) and Ethan (1). Moreover, in the Hebrew Bible thirty-four psalms have no title at all, and for that reason they are known as "orphans." In all, seventy-three psalms bear the title leDawid, translated in the Revised Standard Version as "of David." Unfortunately, it is not clear what the preposition le means in this combination. It could mean "for David" or "concerning David," in which case one would think of a poem dedicated to the great king. David was "the favorite of the songs of Israel," to quote the RSV marginal translation at II Sam. 23:1 rather than the adopted translation "the sweet psalmist of Israel." On this view the psalms are Davidic in the sense that David was the favorite figure in the minds of composers, or perhaps they were composed at his orders or under his sponsorship. It may well be that in the earliest period of the collection of the Psalms the superscription leDawid designated psalms that were used in the royal (Davidic) cult, specifically "those psalms which the king was authorized to recite in the festival cult of the Temple."[12]

It is quite clear, however, that eventually the superscription leDawid was taken to mean "belonging to David" in the sense that the songs in question were composed by David. Clearly this view was held at the time thirteen of these psalms (Ps. 3; 7; 18; 34; 51; 52; 54; 56; 57; 59; 60; 63; 142) were introduced with notes indicating when David supposedly composed or recited the psalm. A good example is the well-known penitential Psalm 51 which bears this superscription: "A psalm of David, when Nathan the prophet came to him, after he had gone in to Bathsheba" (cf. II Sam. 12). Since the conclusion contains a prayer for rebuilding the walls of Jerusalem (Ps. 51:18-19), the psalm in its present form must come from a time much later than David. In the late Old Testament period there was a tendency to ascribe more and more psalms to situations in David's life; and eventually, as we have seen, the whole Psalter was associated with the great name of David.[13] For Israel, this ascription did not necessarily indicate authorship; rather, it signified that the community identified itself with David as it came before God in worship. David was an archetypal figure whose career portrayed both the misery and the grandeur of the People of God. Therefore, as Christoph Barth points out, the people remembered "the king, pursued and abandoned in innocence and guilt, but always delivered and restored to power by the faithfulness of God, in whom their own existence as the People of God had found an expression that was valid for all time."[14] In a troubled time when Israel had no king, the people found in the story of David not only the archetype of its own existence but also the prototype of the coming King who would inaugurate God's kingdom.

THE SETTING OF THE PSALMS IN WORSHIP

The question of the authorship of the psalms fades into insignificance before the larger question of the "cultic" use of psalms, that is, their place and function in worship.

A small clue to the cultic use of the psalms is found in the enigmatic word *selah* which appears here and there (Ps. 3:2, 8; 9:16, 20; etc.). Possibly the term indicated a break or interlude in the recitation of the psalm, at which time the choir or instrumental accompanists would provide an intermezzo. In any case, the psalms were intended to be sung. This is evidenced by other musical notations, such as the instructions found at the head of Psalm 22: "To the choirmaster: according to The Hind of the Dawn." The curious words "The Hind of the Dawn" may refer to the tune to which the psalm was to be sung. The various directions on how the psalms were to be sung were added later, of course, but they emphasize the place of the psalms in the setting of worship.

This brings us to an important point. The main question to ask about any psalm is not the situation in the life of David or in the life of some unknown individual which occasioned the composition. Nor is it essential to try to discover the historical situation in the life of the people Israel in which the psalm was composed, for with the exception of Psalm 137, which clearly presupposes life in Babylonian exile, there are very few historical hints for dating individual psalms. Rather, the important question is the purpose of the psalm, and usually this question leads to an inquiry into the psalm's *situation in worship*. To be sure, not every psalm was composed for use in public worship. Psalm 45, for instance, is a secular ode intended for a royal wedding. But by and large, the psalms belong within the setting of Israel's worship. The psalmists blend their voices in the chorus of the People of God, who respond to God's presence or God's absence in their ongoing historical pilgrimage. Therefore the psalms in which *Israel* speaks to God are also intended *for us* who find ourselves caught up in the dramatic story of God's people.

In recent decades the approach to the psalms in terms of

their function and setting in worship has led to an exciting rediscovery of their meaning. The major pioneers in this rediscovery have been the German scholar Hermann Gunkel and the Scandinavian scholar Sigmund Mowinckel.[15] In this approach, which will be followed in the ensuing chapters of this book, there are two fundamental interests. First, psalms are classified according to literary type or genre. For instance, is a particular psalm a hymn intended to praise God for who God is and for what God has done? Or is it a lament in which a suppliant cries to God for deliverance? And secondly, psalms are considered in terms of their setting in the worship of the People of God. Thus the *form* in which a psalm is cast is related to the *situation* in which it functions. Again the analogy to a modern church hymnbook may be helpful. Songs in a hymnal may be classified according to type (e.g., songs of adoration, of penitence, of thanksgiving, of trust), and also according to their place in the worship service or their use during one of the festivals of the church year (e.g., Christmas, Easter, Pentecost).

This "form-critical" approach to the Psalter, though it minimizes the importance of questions concerning the exact date and circumstances of the composition of a psalm, has helped to bring about a great reversal of judgment about the age of the psalms as a whole. It was not many years ago that scholars, having abandoned the Davidic authorship of the Psalter, were saying that the vast majority of the psalms are very late: postexilic, if not Maccabean. Today, however, many scholars insist that relatively few psalms come from the postexilic period, the period of the Second Temple. Although the Psalter received its final form in that late period, the psalms, for the most part, were used originally in the Temple services during the preexilic period (from David to the fall of the First Temple: 1000 to 587 B.C.).

THE PSALMS AS PRAYED POETRY

Before we turn our attention to the psalms according to their literary type and liturgical setting, a special word should be said about the poetry of the psalms. Considering that the psalms were intended to be recited and sung to musical accompaniment, it is not surprising that they are cast in a poetic form whose exalted style, rhythmic cadences, interplay of imagery, and overtones of thought and feeling come through to the sensitive reader even in English translation. In ancient Israel the rhythm of worship involved not only poetic expression but bodily movement, as in the case of Miriam, who "with timbrels and dancing" sang to Yahweh (Ex. 15:20-21), or David, who with "all the house of Israel" danced and sang to the accompaniment of musical instruments as the Ark was escorted to Jerusalem (II Sam. 6:5). Contemporary expressions of worship in the form of the dance, perhaps to the accompaniment of a guitar, are quite in harmony with the worship presupposed in the psalms!

The rhythm of worship is evident in the poetic structure of a psalm. Unlike our hymnody, Hebrew poetry is not governed by a sense of rhyme. Moreover, there is no consistent attempt to arrange every psalm into carefully measured stanzas, though sometimes a psalm is divided by recurring refrains (e.g., Ps. 46:7, 11; 80:3, 7, 19). Hebrew poetry has meter, to be sure, but the primary characteristic is "a rhythm of sense," as it has been called. The poetry is structured according to "poetic parallelism," that is, the first line is balanced by a corresponding line. The second line illuminates the first, and it does this in one of several ways:

a. Sometimes the second line echoes the same theme in slightly different language:

The earth belongs to Yahweh and everything in it,
the world and those who dwell therein.
—Psalm 24:1

    b. Or the second line strengthens an affirmation by contrasting it with the opposite:

For Yahweh knows the way of the righteous,
but the way of the wicked will perish.
—Psalm 1:6

    c. Or the second line continues the thought by ascending toward its completion:

For Yahweh is a great God
and a great King transcending all gods.
—Psalm 95:3

    Examination of the poetry of the psalms in terms of style, however, could lead no farther than to the conclusion that Israel shared literary patterns with its neighbors in the ancient Near East. As we shall see in the next chapter, archaeological research has shown how heavily indebted Israel was to the surrounding culture, especially to the Canaanites, whose poetic style and imagery are evident in many psalms (e.g., Ps. 18; 29; 68). The poetry of the psalms, however, is distinctive by virtue of its special function in the Israelite setting of worship and its power to speak for the people as they come before God in times of distress, of thankful celebration, and of hymnic jubilation.

    To appreciate the poetic inspiration of the psalms it is important to give attention not only to their literary forms and metric rhythms but also to the imagery and metaphors that are used. The psalmists press human language to its poetic limits in order to give expression to the depth dimension of human life in all its joy and agony, its splendor and misery, its wonder and frustration. As poets the psalmists speak to all people who will listen, in whatever time, place, or circumstance. Their poetic role prompts them to conceal their individuality, even when they speak most forcefully as individuals. They are not concerned with telling us about the details of their personal life or disclosing their inner experiences. As individuals they recede into anonymity. Often they use conventional imagery derived from tradition, such as the ancient chaos myth. Their intention by receding into the background, however, is not to speak impersonally but to let the personal meaning of human life in relation to God burst forth with creative power through poetic language. Human language is used metaphorically to portray experiences that are typical of all people, in whatever time or place they may live. The psalms are "prayed poetry" (Westermann).

It is no wonder, then, that down through the centuries people have made the words of the psalms their own. All that is required, as Roland Murphy reminds us, is "a certain sensitivity to poetry, a yielding to the imagery." Quoting a statement of the noted Catholic theologian Karl Rahner to the effect that "the poetic words and the poetic ear" are the prerequisite for hearing the word of God in the human words of the Bible, Murphy goes on to say: "The poetic is 'prerequisite' in that there is an innate poetic potential in all of us to react to reality by means of imagery."[16] Because the psalmists speak poetically they speak to us—and for us. The deep within them calls out to the deep within us. They articulate the human cry of every person "out of the depths."

NOTES

1. W. H. Auden, "For the Time Being: A Christmas Oratorio," *The Collected Poetry of W. H. Auden* (Random House, 1945), p. 411.
2. Claus Westermann, *The Praise of God in the Psalms*, 2d ed., trans. Keith R. Crim (John Knox Press, 1965), p. 10.
3. Dietrich Bonhoeffer, *Psalms: The Prayer Book of the Bible*, trans. J. A. Burtness (Augsburg Publishing House, 1970).
4. Amos N. Wilder, *The Language of the Gospel* (Harper & Row, 1964), Ch. 1, esp. p. 24.
5. Christoph Barth, *Introduction to the Psalms*, trans. R. A. Wilson (Charles Scribner's Sons, 1966), p. 75.
6. W. T. Davison: "More than any other book of the Old Testament it [the Psalter] has been baptized into Christ." Quoted by John Paterson, *The Praises of Israel* (Charles Scribner's Sons, 1950), p. 7.
7. H. Richard Niebuhr, *The Meaning of Revelation* (Macmillan Co., 1941), Ch. 2.
8. The figure of speech is from Pius Drijvers, *The Psalms: Their Structure and Meaning* (Herder & Herder, 1965), p. 10. However, I do not join with Drijvers in support of the so-called "fuller sense" *(sensus plenior)*, that is, the view that God's revelation in Jesus Christ has disclosed "a new spiritual meaning which is the full depth of what, in germ, lies buried under the surface meaning of the text" (p. 12).
9. See, for instance, Theodor H. Gaster, ed. and trans., *The Dead Sea Scriptures in English Translation* (Doubleday & Co., Anchor Books, 1956), pp. 123-202. The archaeological discovery of the Qumran library began in 1947.
10. Deviations from the Hebrew numerical tradition of the Psalter are discussed by J. A. Sanders, *The Dead Sea Psalms Scroll* (Cornell University Press, 1967).
11. *The Book of Common Prayer*, According to the Use of The Episcopal Church (Seabury Press, 1977), pp. 583-584.
12. Artur Weiser, *The Psalms, A Commentary*, trans. Herbert Hartwell, The Old Testament Library (Westminster Press, 1962), p. 96.
13. Peter R. Ackroyd observes (*Doors of Perception: A Guide to Reading the Psalms* [SCM Press, 1978], pp. 35-36, 74-76) that spaces were left in ancient Hebrew manuscripts of the books of Samuel so that, at that point, readers could consider a psalm that was relevant to the career of David.
14. Christoph Barth, *Introduction to the Psalms*, pp. 64-65.
15. Hermann Gunkel's monumental work *Einleitung in die Psalmen* (2d ed., 1933) has not yet been translated; however, an essay in which

he classifies psalms according to type is available: *The Psalms: A Form-Critical Introduction* (Fortress Press, Facet Books, 1967). For Sigmund Mowinckel's study of the cultic role of the psalms, see *The Psalms in Israel's Worship*, Vols. I-II, trans. D. R. Ap-Thomas (Abingdon Press, 1962).

16. Roland E. Murphy, *The Psalms, Job*, Proclamation Commentaries (Fortress Press, 1977), pp. 12-13.

2
ENTHRONED
ON THE PRAISES
OF ISRAEL

The psalms, as we have seen, are the songs that accompany the People of God on their journey through history. In the Hebrew language these songs are called *tehillim*, "songs of praise." Strictly speaking, this title should be reserved for the type of psalm labeled "hymn" (to be considered in Chapter 5). Indeed, the one time the title occurs in the superscriptions to the psalms it is applied to a hymnic form (Ps. 145). Yet in a larger sense it is appropriate that the title "songs of praise" was finally applied to the Psalter as a whole, which includes a variety of types of psalms: hymns, laments, thanksgivings, songs of trust, wisdom meditations, and others. For the truth is that every psalm, whatever its literary type and whatever its relation to the cult, is actually a song that extols and glorifies God. In one of the most poignant laments of the psalter, Psalm 22, the psalmist affirms that Yahweh is "enthroned on the praises of Israel" (v. 3).

Before we consider the major types of psalms it is necessary to inquire into the *basis* of Israel's worship. True, the psalms are the responses of the worshiping community to the initiative of God. Israel's praise is a reflex of the prior action of God which moves people, as one psalmist testifies, to seek God's "face" (Ps. 27:8), that is, to visit the Temple. At the beginning of his *Confessions*, Augustine strikes this biblical note of the priority of God's initiative:

*Thou movest us to delight in praising Thee; for Thou hast
formed us for Thyself, and our hearts are restless till they find
rest in Thee.*[1]

But the question is: How is God's initiative manifested?
What kind of experience awakens the impulse to praise?

INFLUENCES FROM ISRAEL'S ENVIRONMENT

This question about the basis of Israel's worship has
received considerable attention in recent decades. Thanks
to the light cast by archaeology upon the culture of the
ancient Near East, we have become increasingly aware of
Israel's profound indebtedness to the ritual and mythology of its neighbors. When the Israelites settled in the Land
of Canaan during the two centuries before David (ca.
1200-1000 B.C.), they became part of an advanced culture
where forms of worship were already firmly established.
This was true especially at places like Shechem, Bethel,
and Jerusalem which had been Canaanite sanctuaries for
centuries before they were taken over by Israel and
converted to the worship of Yahweh. Beth-el literally
means "house of El." El was the high god of the Canaanite
pantheon, the "Father" of the gods, and the "Creator of
creatures," as we know from mythological tablets found
on the coast of Syria at Ras Shamra (ancient Ugarit), dating
from about 1400 B.C.

Israel did not say a flat No of repudiation to the
advanced culture into which it entered but rather said No
and Yes. Faith in Yahweh, the God of Israel, demanded
turning from other "gods" and, consequently, challeng-
ing the theological presuppositions of the religions of the
environment. These religions, with their elaborate myth
and ritual, enabled people to find meaning and security
within the order of creation which moves serenely in the
rhythms of seedtime and harvest, summer and winter, life

and death (Gen. 8:22). The modern counterpart would be a religion that diverts people from the conflicts and terrors of history and promises the peace which comes with integration into the natural order, "the peace of nature." Israel's faith, however, perceived divine reality in the dynamic arena of social change; hence, the first response to the religions of the environment was critical. There could be no compromise between faith in Yahweh and the gods of paganism. However, Israel's No at this deepest level was usually accompanied by a Yes of appropriation, that is, by taking over forms of worship (such as sacrifice) and literary forms (such as the psalm) and converting them to the service of Yahweh. The three great agricultural festivals of the Canaanites were adopted, and eventually were adapted to decisive events in Israel's historical experience. "Three times in the year you shall keep a feast to me," was the command from Yahweh in Ex. 23:14, and as the context shows, these were the festival times of the Canaanite agricultural calendar (on the festivals, see Chapter 6).

The situation that Israel faced in Canaan was like many situations faced by the Christian community as it has moved into alien cultures and has had to decide whether to adopt native forms of religious expression. This problem was vividly illustrated some years ago, when the author was teaching for a summer in a theological institute held in Ghana. A heated discussion arose as to whether the Christian churches should admit into their worship the rhythms of African drums and folk dances that were part of the native religion and communal life of the people. Some of the older generation, under the influence of the first missionary churches, opposed this radical step, knowing that the African drum "talks" its own languages (war, sex, native religion, etc.). Members of the younger generation, however, believed that the risks of using the drum and dance in worship were worth taking for the sake of letting the Christian faith become indigenous. Thus, in ever new ways the People of God have had to face the problem of reexpressing faith in the forms provided by different cultures.

This problem became crucial in the Old Testament period when Israelite leaders made the fateful decision to ask for a king to rule them "like all the nations" (I Sam. 8:4-22). The step was risky, as the prophet Samuel pointed out, for concentration of power in a king would deprive the people of their cherished liberties. But there was also a theological danger, for, as recent studies in the "sacral kingship" of the ancient Near East have shown, the king was thought to be endowed with divine talents and to enjoy a special relationship with the deity. To adopt kingship, then, was not only to run a political danger; it was to take the chance that "court poetry" of the ancient world would erode the Israelite faith in Yahweh which received its classical and most vigorous expression in the time when Israel had no king. Liberal elements, however, insisted that Yahweh was leading the people forward into the new way of life and thought represented by the monarchy (see Chapter 6). Thus, the kingdom established by David and consolidated by his son Solomon was characterized by a new openness to cultural influences from Egypt, Mesopotamia, and elsewhere.

ISRAEL'S DEBT TO ITS NEIGHBORS

Therefore the songs that were used in the worship services of the Jerusalem Temple should be viewed in the wider context of the psalm literature of the ancient Near East: the Sumerians, Babylonians, Canaanites, and Egyptians. The psalms in Israel's psalter are similar in form, and often in content, to the hymns and laments composed by Israel's neighbors. As an example we may take the following passage from a hymn to the

Moon-God, *Sin,* which archaeologists found at the site of Nineveh, an ancient capital of the Assyrian empire. In its present form it dates from about the time of Jeremiah (seventh century B.C.), but the tablet states that it was *ANET 385* copied from an older edition.

> *O Lord, decider of the destinies of heaven and earth, whose word no one alters,*
> *Who controls water and fire, leader of living creatures, what god is like thee?*
> *In heaven who is exalted? Thou! Thou alone art exalted.*
> *On earth who is exalted? Thou! Thou alone art exalted.*
> *Thou! When thy word is pronounced in heaven the Igigi prostrate themselves.*
> *Thou! When thy word is pronounced on earth the Anunnaki kiss the ground.*
> *Thou! When thy word drifts along in heaven like the wind it makes rich the feeding and drinking of the land.*
> *Thou! When thy word settles down on the earth green vegetation is produced.*
> *Thou! Thy word makes fat the sheepfold and the stall; it makes living creatures widespread.*
> *Thou! Thy word causes truth and justice to be, so that the people speak the truth.*
> *Thou! Thy word which is far away in heaven, which is hidden in the earth is something no one sees.*
> *Thou! Who can comprehend thy word, who can equal it?*
> *O Lord, in heaven as to dominion, on earth as to valor, among the gods thy brothers, thou hast not a rival.*[2]

Compare the language of this hymn with passages from Israel's psalms that raise the question: "Who is like thee, O Yahweh, among the gods?" (Ex. 15:11; Ps. 86: 8-10; and especially Ps. 89:5-14).

We may take a step farther. Not only are there striking formal similarities to the songs of Israel's neighbors but in a few instances Israel has taken over hymns from the

Canaanite environment (just as the church has borrowed pagan or "secular" melodies and poetry) and used them in the praise of Yahweh. One example is Psalm 29, which is an adaptation of a Canaanite hymn originally sung to Hadad, the god of the storm. In the modified form of the old hymn it is Yahweh whose "voice" is heard in the thunderstorm and who is enthroned above the tumult of nature's forces.

> **The voice of Yahweh is over the waters,**
> **the God of glory thunders,**
> **Yahweh over the mighty waters.**
> **The voice of Yahweh is powerful,**
> **the voice of Yahweh is majestic.**
>
> **The voice of Yahweh breaks the cedars,**
> **Yahweh breaks the cedars of Lebanon.**
> **He makes Lebanon skip around like a calf,**
> **and Sirion [Mount Hermon] like a young wild ox.**
>
> **The voice of Yahweh stirs up flames of fire,**
> **the voice of Yahweh makes the wilderness tremble,**
> **Yahweh causes to tremble the wilderness of Kadesh.**
> **—Psalm 29:3-8**

The poem reaches a climax by announcing Yahweh's kingship over the flood *(mabbûl)*, the mythical waters of chaos (a theme to which we shall return in Chapter 6).

> **Yahweh is enthroned over the flood,**
> **Yahweh is enthroned as king forever!**
> **—Psalm 29:10**

Another striking example of the borrowing of hymnic elements is the superb creation hymn, Psalm 104. It has long been recognized that this psalm, both in form and content, is related to the beautiful "Hymn to the Aton," which was found in a tomb at Tell el-Amarna, Egypt, the capital of the reforming Pharaoh Akh-en-Aton (Amen-hotep IV, ca. 1380-1362 B.C.). The Egyptian hymn expresses the universal beneficence and re-creating power of the sun disc (the Aton). Some scholars maintain that the new style of worship introduced by the iconoclastic Pharaoh was monotheistic. Compare the following excerpt, for instance, with Psalm 104:24:

> *How manifold it is, what thou hast made!*
> *They are hidden from the face (of man).*
> *O sole god, like whom there is no other!*
> *Thou didst create the world according to thy desire,*
> *Whilst thou wert alone:*
> *All men, cattle, and wild beasts,*
> *Whatever is on earth, going upon (its) feet,*
> *And what is on high, flying with its wings.*

And notice how Psalm 104:27-30 echoes the thought of the Egyptian poem that each day is a new creation:

> *The world came into being by thy hand,*
> *According as thou hast made them.*
> *When thou hast risen they live,*
> *When thou settest they die.*
> *Thou art lifetime thy own self,*
> *For one lives (only) through thee.*[3]   ANET 369-373

During the period of the Davidic monarchy this hymn came to be known in Jerusalem, probably through wisdom circles, and was adapted to the worship of Yahweh, the sole Creator and Lord.

Later on (in Chapter 6) we shall have more to say about how the great worship festivals in Jerusalem were influenced by the festivals of Israel's neighbors, such as the New Year festival celebrated in Babylonia. First, however, it is important to focus on what was distinctive in Israel's worship. For, when Israel borrowed literary forms and cultic practices, it did not merely imitate its neighbors. Borrowed forms were transformed, religious practices were converted. This is evident from the examples cited above in which hymns or hymnic motifs appropriated from the religions of the cultural environment have been recast for Israel's liturgical use.

ISRAEL'S PRAISE IN MINOR AND MAJOR KEYS

It would not be surprising if modern people would attempt, like Akhenaton, to turn to the sun disc or some other cosmic phenomenon to symbolize their worship of the Power behind the whole cosmic order. For in modern times the notion has developed—perhaps in a more radical fashion than at any other time in human history—that "God" is outside our historical world. Few people who go to synagogue or church today expect God to be actively involved in the human world: the civil rights struggle, the war against poverty and oppression, the tragic suffering in Africa or India, or the harsh political realities of the strife between the great world powers. The popular notion is that God is, if not "up there," at least "out there" somewhere—a transcendent deity "located in some never-never land beyond the universe." For all practical purposes, this God who is "out of this world" is "estranged from the human situation," distant from the places where historical beings are living, suffering, and deciding.[4]

Israel's praise, by contrast, did not begin by extolling the Creator who is before, behind, beyond, and above the whole created order. True, the Psalter contains magnificent creation psalms, like Psalm 104 which has just been mentioned, showing that Israel shared a creation faith with ancient peoples, such as the Egyptians, the Babylonians, and the Canaanites. It is not proper, however, to begin our study with creation psalms for the reason that Israel's worship was not grounded primarily in creation faith. Rather, the invocation to worship was based fundamentally upon a "root experience" of liberation from bondage that was enshrined in the memory of the people.[5]

From early times Israel confessed its faith characteristically by telling the story of its life: "We were once slaves of the mightiest emperor of the day but the Holy God intervened and gave us a future." The ancient confession of faith opens, like a symphony pathétique, in a minor mode: the portrayal of a human situation of oppression and limitation; and this minor strain modulates into the major key of praise to the God who opened a way into the future out of a no-exit situation.

This "root experience," celebrated in worship from the very beginning of Israel's existence as a people, is evident at all stages of tradition. It provides the motive for praise in an old poetic couplet known as the Song of Miriam. This ancient poem may have been composed by one who witnessed the event of the crossing of the sea (not the Red Sea, but a shallow body of water farther north in the area of Lake Timsah, in Hebrew called "the Sea of Reeds"). In any case, it is one of the oldest poetic fragments in the Bible.

> *Sing to Yahweh*
> *for [ki] he has triumphed gloriously,*
> *the horse and his rider*
> *he has hurled into the sea.*
> *—Exodus 15:21*

We have here the literary genre of the "hymn"—the oldest example in the Old Testament. (See Chapter 5 for a fuller discussion of this literary type.) Miriam's hymn begins with an invitation to the community (the verb "sing" is plural in the Hebrew) to join in praise to Yahweh. The transitional word "for" (Hebrew, *ki*) gives the motive for praise. The remainder of the song indicates the basis for worship. It is not some general awareness of God's greatness in the cosmos but rather the experience of God's saving presence in a situation of distress when, humanly speaking, there was no way out—no exodus. It is significant that Israel's history of worship, which reached its climax in the praises of the Psalter, was initiated in that crucial hour at the beginning of the tradition when women, under the leadership of Miriam, sang and danced to music, inviting the people to join them.

Israel's praise to the liberating God is also expressed in an ancient poem, probably from the period of the tribal confederacy that flourished before the rise of the Davidic monarchy, which provides a poetic parallel to the Song of Miriam. The longer poem, composed in Canaanite literary style and filled with Canaanite mythical imagery, praises Yahweh for a historical deed of liberation.

> *Who is like you in the heavenly council, Yahweh?*
> *Who is like you, majestic in holiness?*
> *You who are awesome in deeds, who does wonders?*
> *You stretched out your right hand,*
> *Earth swallowed them.*
> *In your faithfulness you led the people that you redeemed,*
> *You led them in your power to your holy abode.*
> *—Exodus 15:11-13*

The jubilant note of Miriam's song of praise echoed and reechoed from generation to generation as the story of Israel's liberation from bondage was told and retold. The story, found in expanded form in the book of Exodus, chs. 1-15, displays the same structure of oppression and deliverance, humiliation and exaltation that we have noted previously. The exodus story begins with a cry out of distress as it portrays vividly the oppression of Jacob's descendants in Egypt (Ex. 1 and 2). The turning point in the lament comes in connection with the episode of the burning bush.

Then Yahweh said: "I have certainly seen the affliction of my people, and their cry of distress because of their slave drivers I have heard. For I know their sufferings, and have come down to rescue them from the power of the Egyptians, and to escort them out of that land unto a good and spacious land, a land flowing with milk and honey."

—*Exodus 3:7-8a*

The rest of the story is a narrative portrayal of how Yahweh, the God of the ancestors, humbled the mighty and exalted those of low degree (chs. 4-14). The dramatic story, in its present form, reaches a climax with the Song of the Sea, mentioned above.

Thus the exodus story, from beginning to end, is told to praise and glorify the God whose saving power was manifested in creating the historical community known as Israel and in giving the people a future. The story was probably shaped through repetition in liturgical ceremonies, chiefly the observance of the Passover festival.

So crucial was the exodus for Israel's existence as a community of faith that the event was relived and reenacted from generation to generation. In the great festivals the story of the formation of Israel was told and retold: the deliverance from Egypt, the crossing of the Reed Sea, the entrance into Canaan. The story was not related as something "back there" in the past. Rather, the story had a meaning for persons here and now. It was a drama in which the present generation was involved. Even today the Passover ritual contains the reminder that believing Jews should confess that the God of the ancestors brought them, the contemporary generation, out of Egypt.

It was not alone our fathers whom the Holy One, blessed be He, redeemed, but also us whom He redeemed with them, as it is said, *"And us He brought out thence that He might lead us to, and give us, the land which He swore to our fathers."*[6]

The contemporaneity of the exodus story of liberation is evident in a passage found in the book of Deuteronomy —a book that received its present form after the fall of Jerusalem in 587 B.C. The language, therefore, is colored by the relatively late Deuteronomic style. Yet the content, in the judgment of some scholars, is much older.

My ancestor was a wandering Aramean who descended to Egypt. There he sojourned with a small band and there he grew to be a great, powerful and populous nation. But the Egyptians maltreated us, humiliated us, and imposed upon us heavy servitude. Then we cried to Yahweh, the God of our ancestors; and Yahweh heard our cry and saw our affliction, our trouble and our oppression. Yahweh caused us to go out of Egypt with a strong hand and an outstretched arm, with great terror, with signs and wonders; and he brought us to this place and gave us this land, a land flowing with milk and honey.

—Deuteronomy 26:5-9; see also 6:20-23

This "historical credo,"[7] as it has been called, is not a private prayer. It is, rather, a confession of faith that is made in connection with an act of worship: the presentation of the "firstfruits" at the sanctuary at harvesttime (Deut. 26:10). The worshiper who engages in this cultic act of thanksgiving is identified with the worshiping community, as indicated by the plural pronouns ("The Egyptians maltreated *us*"; "*We* cried to Yahweh . . . and Yahweh heard *our* cry"; etc.).

Even more important for our immediate purpose, the passage expresses the motive of Israel's praise—praise that modulates from the minor into the major key. It begins by portraying a situation of distress. "A wandering Aramean" refers to the ancestor Jacob, and if one paraphrases the original Hebrew more exactly, Jacob's wandering is like the "straying" of an animal that has lost its way. The credo continues with a further portrayal of the people's distress in Egypt, out of which "we cried to Yahweh, the God of our ancestors." This cry "out of the depths," however, is followed by the jubilant affirmation that "Yahweh heard our cry and saw our affliction" and marvelously opened a way into the future. Thus the appeal out of distress and the jubilant cry of deliverance combine to express Israel's praise of God.

This pattern—from distress to jubilation, from humiliation to exaltation—can be traced through the whole Bible, especially in liturgical materials. It is found, for instance, in the Song of Deborah (Judg. 5), one of the oldest pieces of Hebrew literature of any length, which praises Yahweh for coming to the rescue of the people in a time of distress when they were threatened by the overwhelming forces of the Canaanites (ca. 1100 B.C.). It is found in the much later Song of Hannah (I Sam. 2:1-10), a psalm of thanksgiving for the community's deliverance from deep troubles. And in the New Testament the language of Hannah's song is echoed in the Magnificat (Luke 1:46-55) in which Mary praises the God who exalts the humble and fills the hungry with good things:

He has shown strength with his arm,
he has scattered the proud in the imagination of
    their hearts,
he has put down the mighty from their thrones,
and exalted those of low degree;
he has filled the hungry with good things,
and the rich he has sent empty away.
He has helped his servant Israel,
in remembrance of his mercy,
as he spoke to our fathers,
to Abraham and to his posterity for ever.
                    —Luke 1:51-55 (RSV)

Also in the religions of other ancient peoples, such as the Babylonians, the gods were regarded as taking part in historical affairs.[8] One of the fundamental differences, however, between Israel's psalms and the songs of its neighbors is that in the context of worship Israel turned primarily to its own historical experience to confess its faith. A psalmist recalls the saving event at the sea (Ex. 14) and the subsequent passage through the Jordan River (Josh. 4):

When Israel came out of Egypt,
  Jacob from a people of outlandish speech,
Judah became his sanctuary,
  Israel his dominion.
The sea looked and ran away;
  Jordan turned back.
The mountains skipped like rams,
  the hills like young sheep.
                    —Psalm 114:1-2 (NEB)

Here the poet uses language that reverberates with mythical overtones of the Divine Warrior's victory over the powers of chaos ("sea"), suggesting that the saving event at the beginning of Israel's history was also a creative event. Israel, the People of God, was created *ex nihilo*—out of the "nothingness" of historical oblivion, the chaos of meaningless oppression. Therefore, Yahweh is praised as Israel's Maker.

Come, let us bow in worship;
  Let us kneel before Yahweh, our Maker!
For Yahweh is our God,
  and we are his people,
    the flock that he shepherds.
                    —Psalm 95:6-7

So crucial was the exodus for Israel's knowledge of God and Israel's understanding of its existence as a people that the story was told and retold in the great religious festivals. Eventually the story was supplemented with the narrative of how Yahweh led Israel out of the tribal form of existence into the "modern" form of the state, by raising up David to be king and by making Jerusalem the chosen sanctuary (Ps. 78).

This confessional way of retelling the Israelite tradition provides a background for the study of a special group of psalms that express the "shared history" of the believing and worshiping community. These "storytelling" or "historical" psalms portray Yahweh's saving action in the history or story of Israel. The story/history is not related with detachment but is told as a drama that is true "for me" or "for us." Since the Christian community has appropriated the story of Israel as its own, it is important to consider what is involved in this kind of narrative praise. Some religions, as Amos Wilder reminds us, emphasize philosophical reflection, others mystical meditation, and still others didactic discourse; but "the narrative mode is uniquely important in Christianity."

> It is through the Christian story that God speaks, and all heaven and earth come into it. God is an active and purposeful God and his action with and for men has a beginning, a middle and an end like any good story. The life of a Christian is not like a dream shot through with visions and illuminations, but a pilgrimage, a race, in short, a history. The new Christian speech inevitably took the form of a story.[9]

The "narrative" mode is evident throughout the Psalter, especially in a number of psalms in which Israel's praise takes the form of recounting Yahweh's "deeds of salvation" (e.g., Ps. 66:5-7; 71:15-16; 75:1; 77:11-15; 98:1-3; 107:31-32; 145:4-6). In a group of "storytelling psalms"—sometimes called "salvation history psalms"—the central subject is the recitation of Yahweh's "mighty deeds" in Israel's history. One gets the impression from reading and contemplating these psalms that they have a strong didactic interest: history is recounted in order to *teach* people the meaning of their history. These psalms retell the story of the People of God to show God's *faithfulness*, even when the people "have erred and strayed" from the path "like lost sheep" and "have followed too much the devices and desires of [their] own hearts"—to quote the well-known words of the Prayer of General Confession.

It is recommended that these psalms be read in the following order:

{	Psalm 105	A historical summary paralleling the Pentateuch from Genesis 12 on.
	Psalm 106	A similar summary recited in a penitential mood.
	Psalm 78	A summary that carries the story up to the selection of David and the choice of Mt. Zion (Jerusalem), again recited in a penitential style.
{	Psalm 135	A historical summary that includes a reference to Yahweh's power as creator (vs. 5–7).
	Psalm 136	An antiphonal summary of Yahweh's great deeds, beginning with the creation.

In the present form of the Psalter, the first two psalms bracketed together (Ps. 105 and Ps. 106) are regarded as Hallelujah Psalms, that is, each begins and ends with the cultic exclamation, "Praise Yahweh."

[The Hallelujah at the end of Psalm 104 actually belongs at the beginning of Psalm 105. Psalm 135 is also a hallelujah psalm, while Psalm 136 is a *todah* ("thanksgiving") psalm, as is clear from its beginning and end.]

Here, however, we are not chiefly concerned with how these psalms were classified in the final edition of the Psalter or with their proper classification according to literary type (e.g., "hymn" or "song of thanksgiving"). The important thing is their subject matter. These five psalms recapitulate the unfolding drama of Yahweh's dealings with the people from the very beginning of Israel's history to the entrance into the Promised Land and—in the case of Psalm 78—as far as the raising up of David as "the anointed one." They recite events fundamental to Israel's self-understanding as a people and essential to Israel's knowledge of who God is.

This historical accent in the Psalter holds the possibility of bringing these songs of worship closer to where we live. We too are historical beings, and if we are to know God at all, our knowledge will be a historical knowledge. As H. Richard Niebuhr has reminded us: "We are in history as the fish is in water and what we mean by the revelation of God can be indicated only as we point through the medium in which we live."[10] The Christian church has inherited this historical legacy, minus the nationalistic overtones that sounded at times in Israel's scriptures. In the New Testament, too, the church speaks of God primarily by telling the story of Jesus Christ, a story that is understood to be part of the larger story of God's dealings with the people Israel.[11]

The last pair of psalms bracketed together (Ps. 135 and Ps. 136) has one noteworthy feature in common: each associates the story of Yahweh's deeds on behalf of Israel with Yahweh's actions as creator in the beginning. This is true especially of Psalm 136, a historical recitation of Yahweh's mighty deeds, in which the congregation makes an antiphonal response to each affirmation:

For his faithfulness endures for ever!

(See II Chron. 7:3-6, where we find the worshiping congregation responding with this refrain.) Whereas in the first pair the recitation begins with the exodus (Ps. 106) or with Abraham, Isaac, and Jacob (Ps. 105—the only direct reference to the patriarchs in the Psalter), in Psalm 136 the community traces the actions of God right back to the beginning: to God's first work of creating the world (vs. 4-9). This is Israel's way of saying that the meaning disclosed in its own historical experience ("the story of our life") unveils the meaning that underlies the whole of human history right from the start, and indeed of the entire cosmos. The "word" that Yahweh spoke to Israel is the same word by which the heavens and the earth were made (Ps. 33:6-9). (See previous discussion, pp. 46-66, and Chapter 5.)

CRIES OUT OF A SITUATION OF DISTRESS

These psalms in the "narrative" mode show that the recapitulation of the story of God's action in the history of the people Israel was not just a paraphrase of the story found in the Pentateuch. Rather, in worship the story was *retold* with a contemporaneous ring, so that it touched the concerns of people in their present situation. It is one thing to affirm that God has done marvelous things in the past. For many worshipers, however, the problem is that, if God was marvelously active in the past, why is God apparently inactive in the present, when people find themselves in deep distress? This is a perennial problem for faith. In the Psalter such distress finds expression in laments in which psalmists, perplexed about the meaning of the present, seek consolation by recalling God's mighty deeds in the past. This is the case in an individual lament:

I will consider the deeds of Yahweh,
yes, I will recall your wonders of long ago.

I will meditate on all your work,
will ponder your actions.
O God, your way is holy.
What deity is great like our God?
You are the God who works miracles;
you have displayed your power among the peoples.
With your mighty arm you redeemed your people,
the children of Jacob and Joseph.

—Psalm 77:11-15

The same note is sounded in community laments, like this
one:

O God, with our own ears we have heard,
our ancestors have recounted to us,
the deeds you performed in their time,
what your hand did in days long ago.
You expelled nations, but them you planted;
peoples you afflicted, but them you made whole.
For not by their sword did they gain the land,
nor by their arm did they win victory;
but your right hand, your mighty arm,
and the light of your countenance;
for you were well-disposed toward them.

—Psalm 44:1-3

Some readers may discount the latter lament on the
ground that Israel as a nation had experienced a
humiliating defeat at the hand of a political power and was
disillusioned because God had not come to Israel's rescue,
as in days past when the people were victimized by
Pharaoh's tyranny. Such a community lament, it is
argued, could be raised by a modern nation which
supposes naively that "God is on our side" and which
feels "let down" in the political contests of history. Is the
problem so simple, however? Even when we make due

allowances for the nationalism in some of the psalms, there is the larger problem that the People of God *(which is not essentially a nation)* must live through times of uncertainty when history appears to be under the control of powers of evil and darkness. Even in the perspective of faith, the sovereignty of God is hidden, the meaning of human history unclear. Out of such experiences arises the poignant question of whether God has forgotten the people or disregarded human cries of suffering. Israel's lament, raised in a time of exile by an uprooted and despondent people, is typical of the cries raised by many people who feel the brutal weight of oppression and injustice:

> *My way is hidden from Yahweh,*
> *my plight is ignored by my God.*
> —Isaiah 40:27b

Just because Israel believed so firmly in God's presence in history, the people had to learn to sing praises, not only in times of God's presence but in trying times of God's absence.

Perhaps we can begin to understand, then, why so many of Israel's psalms are laments. More than one third of the psalms fall into the category of complaints to God in a situation of limitation and threat (see Chapter 3). Indeed, it is striking that all the psalms that have superscriptions referring to episodes in David's life are laments! Just as Israel in the time of Egyptian oppression cried out for deliverance when the opposing powers were formidable and there was no hope, so in the course of Israel's historical pilgrimage the people again and again cried out to God from the depth of their distress—in the name of David in whom Israel found its existence before God portrayed.

Israel's cries "out of the depths" were not based on the philosophical kind of atheism that has come to be familiar in the modern period. Now and then psalmists speak about the "fool" who says in his heart, "there is no God" (Ps. 14:1; cf. 10:4). But this is a practical, not a theoretical atheism. The fool does not deny God's reality; he only denies that God's action affects his life. He thinks that God does not see and therefore he can live as he pleases (Ps. 10:11). Helmer Ringgren draws attention in this connection to the old Babylonian phrase "living *ina ramâni-shu*"—"living by oneself, on one's own resources, without dependence on God." This refusal to "let God be God" is "the essence of sin" and hence the fool and his folly will be exposed in the day when God judges the people.[12]

GOD'S FAITHFULNESS

As can be seen from the narrative psalms treated above, a fundamental theme of Israel's praise is God's faithfulness. One of the key words in the psalms is the Hebrew word *ḥesed*, which is rendered variously: "mercy" (KJV), "steadfast love" (RSV), "constancy, love" (NEB), "love" (JB, NIV). *Ḥesed* refers to the faithfulness that characterizes God's covenant relationship with the people or, vice versa, that should characterize the relationship of the people to their God. The term is filled with the rich content of personal relationship, as in the friendship between David and Jonathan, though it also suggests a relationship in which a stronger party can offer help and protection to the weaker (see the story in I Sam. 20, where David shows *ḥesed*, loyalty to his friend).[13] Notice that when the term is used of God in the psalms it is often paralleled with such words as "goodness" (Ps. 23:6), "salvation" (Ps. 85:7), "faithfulness" (Ps. 89:2; 100:5), "righteousness" (Ps. 103:17), "truth" (Ps. 25:5). Unlike the capricious gods of the ancient world, the God whom Israel worships is true to promises made, constant in faithfulness, consistent in behavior.

Yet in the complexities and perplexities of human life the purpose of God can be seen only dimly. There is no sure evidence to prove that God is in control beyond the shadow of a doubt. Hence the psalmists often cried to God out of their distress, remembering how God had manifested favor (*hesed*) in the past and hoping that God would once again "show his face" graciously. Their lament was a form of praise based on the conviction that God is concerned about the people's condition and answers the human cry in ways surpassing human expectation:

Make your ways known to me, Yahweh;
  teach me your paths.
Let me walk in your truth and teach me,
  for you are the God who saves me;
  for you I have waited all day long.
Consider your compassion and your faithfulness, Yahweh!
  for they have continued from ages past.
Don't consider the errors and sins of my youth,
  rather, consider me according to your faithfulness,
    for your goodness' sake, Yahweh!

                      —Psalm 25:4-7

Many of the psalms, like the alphabetical (acrostic) psalm just quoted, express the stance of "waiting" for God—waiting for the time when the reality of God's presence and the sovereignty of God's purpose in the world will once again become clear. The present is often the time of "the eclipse of God," to quote the title of a book by the Jewish philosopher Martin Buber. In the time of the exile, when many Israelites thought that God had deserted them, a prophet echoed the note of waiting struck in many psalms of lament:

Even the young may tire and faint
and the strong may fall exhausted;

but those who wait for Yahweh will renew their vitality;
they will mount on wings like eagles;
they will run without getting weary,
they will walk and not faint.

—Isaiah 40:30-31

In our time, too, we can understand this waiting for God, this experience of God's seeming absence from the human situation. It is more difficult for us to understand that Israel's lament out of distress was a way of praising God—in the time of God's absence.

In the following discussion we shall not begin with hymns that praise God's greatness in general terms as the Ruler of universal history or the Creator of heaven and earth. We shall turn, first, to Israel's speech to God in the form of lament. Since this type of psalm quickly resolves into the assurance that Yahweh hears the human cry, we shall turn next to the songs of thanksgiving. Then in later chapters we shall study the hymns that extol the greatness and glory of God, who is enthroned as King over Israel, the nations, and the entire creation.

NOTES

1. *The Confessions of Saint Augustine,* trans. J. G. Pilkington (Liveright Publishing Corp., 1943), Bk. 2, Ch. 1.
2. "Hymn to the Moon-God," trans. Ferris J. Stephens, in James B. Pritchard (ed.), *Ancient Near Eastern Texts Relating to the Old Testament,* 3d ed. (Princeton University Press, 1969), pp. 385-386. In this hymn the "Igigi" are the great gods of heaven; the "Anunnaki" are the gods of the earth and the netherworld.
3. "Hymn to the Aton," trans. John A. Wilson in Pritchard, *Ancient Near Eastern Texts,* pp. 369-373.
4. These lines are influenced by a paper presented by the late Arthur C. McGill, "A Theological Criticism of 'Transcendence,'" at the Society of The Biblical Theologians, Nov. 17, 1967.
5. See especially Emil Fackenheim, *God's Presence in History: Jewish*

Affirmations and Philosophical Reflections (New York University Press, 1970). Fackenheim observes that Jewish tradition reaches back to two "root experiences" of the Mosaic period: "the saving experience" (Exodus) and "the commanding experience" (Sinai).

6. David and Tamar de Sola Pool (eds.), *The Haggadah of the Passover* (Bloch Publishing Co., 1953), p. 51.

7. See Gerhard von Rad, "The Form-Critical Problem of the Hexateuch," in *The Problem of the Hexateuch and Other Essays,* trans. E. W. T. Dicken (McGraw-Hill Book Co., 1966), pp. 1-78. Von Rad's view is summarized in *Genesis, A Commentary,* rev. ed., The Old Testament Library (Westminster Press, 1973), pp. 13-23.

8. See Bertil Albrektson, *History and the Gods: An Essay on the Idea of Historical Events as Divine Manifestations in the Ancient Near East and in Israel* (Lund: C. W. K. Gleerup, 1967). Albrektson, at the end of his study, notes the peculiar way that Yahweh's acts in history were remembered and celebrated in the Israelite cult.

9. Amos N. Wilder, *The Language of the Gospel* (Harper & Row, 1964), pp. 64-65.

10. H. Richard Niebuhr, *The Meaning of Revelation* (Macmillan Co., 1941), p. 48.

11. The current emphasis on "story-telling theology" is discussed, e.g., by George W. Stroup, *The Promise of Narrative Theology* (John Knox Press, 1982), and Michael Goldberg, *Theology and Narrative: A Critical Introduction* (Abingdon Press, 1982).

12. Helmer Ringgren, *The Faith of the Psalmists* (Fortress Press, 1963), p. 35.

13. For a thorough, illuminating discussion of this important Hebrew term, see Katharine D. Sakenfeld, *The Meaning of Ḥesed in the Hebrew Bible,* Harvard Semitic Monographs 17 (Scholars Press, 1978). See further her forthcoming book *Faithfulness in Action: Loyalty in Biblical Lifestyle* (Fortress Press, Overture Series).

3
THE TRIALS
OF FAITH

Israel's praise was evoked by the action of the God who turned to a band of oppressed slaves and in a marvelous way opened to them a new possibility of life. Accordingly, the faith of the psalmists does not rest upon glittering generalities about the nature of God or upon a numinous awareness of God's transcendent majesty in the remote reaches of the cosmos; rather, it is founded upon the good news that the Holy God becomes present in the midst of history to help those who are oppressed.

> Yahweh achieves vindication
> and justice for all the oppressed.
> He manifested his ways to Moses,
> his actions to the Israelites.
> —Psalm 103:6-7

Here the psalmist alludes to the story in Exodus 33 and 34, where, in a problematic situation, Moses asked for a manifestation of Yahweh's "ways" (Ex. 33:13) and received the assurance that, despite the people's fickle behavior, Yahweh would nevertheless go with them and give them a future. The marvelous demonstration of Yahweh's faithfulness (ḥesed), greater than anything expected or deserved, provides the motive for the imperatives that summon the people to worship: "Sing!"

"Make a joyful noise!" etc. Claus Westermann observes that in contrast to Babylonian psalms, "something entirely new has been added to the psalms of praise in the Old Testament: the imperative exhortation to praise."[1] This is because Israel has a special story to tell.

The story of Yahweh's turning toward a people in distress, as found in the exodus tradition (Ex. 1-15), is supplemented with the narrative of Israel's murmurings in the wilderness. According to traditions found in the books of Exodus (Ex. 16; 17; and 32), Numbers (Num. 11; 14; 16; 20; 21), and Deuteronomy (e.g., Deut. 8), the wilderness sojourn was the time when Israel's faith was put to the test. To be sure, "signs" of Yahweh's presence were given, such as the manna that fell from the desert bushes, the quails that drifted into the area with the prevailing winds, or the water that was found in unexpected places. These signs, however, were indications but not proofs of God's presence and guidance. Indeed, the period in the wilderness was a time when the people longed for the "fleshpots" of Egypt and when they murmured, "Is Yahweh among us or not?" (Ex. 17:7).

This portrayal of Israel in the wilderness was not so much a recital of ancient history as a mirror in which the people found its own history with God reflected. In the same mirror the pilgrim People of God of the New Testament period saw itself. Paul, for instance, did not dismiss the events of the wilderness as ancient history but insisted that "these things . . . were written down for our instruction, upon whom the end of the ages has come" (I Cor. 10:11). The signs given to God's people by Christ were not proofs of God's real presence and sovereign control of history beyond any shadow of a doubt; they were assurances given to faith. Still it must be said, even in the time that Christians mark as A.D. (i.e., after Christ): "We walk by faith, not by sight" (II Cor. 5:7).

It is not surprising, then, that the Bible contains a great deal of literature of lament. Embedded in The Book of Jeremiah are six "confessions" or laments in which the prophet complains to God in strong language, protests his innocence, and cries out for vindication over his enemies:

1. Jer. 11:18–12:6   "A lamb led to the slaughter"
2. Jer. 15:10-21   "I sat alone"
3. Jer. 17:14-18   "Be not a terror to me"
4. Jer. 18:19-23   "Is evil a recompense for good?"
5. Jer. 20:7-13   "A fire shut up in my bones"
6. Jer. 20:14-18   "Why did I come forth from the womb?"

A good example is the second lament (Jer. 15:10-21). Like Hamlet, Jeremiah castigates his mother for having given birth to him (cf. Job 3, a similar passage); he cries out for vengeance upon his persecutors; he accuses God of having become like a "deceitful brook" that is full during the spring rains but dries up in the summer; and at the end he is given an oracle in which Yahweh assures him of deliverance.

The fact that Jeremiah raised such cries of dereliction gave rise to the later tradition that he was the author of the mournful poems in Lamentations, composed in the shadow of the destruction of Jerusalem by the Babylonians in 587 B.C. Three of these poems (Lam. 1; 2; 4) are really funeral dirges which open with the customary wail 'ekah (translated "how," e.g., Lam. 1:1) and are cast in the "limping 3/2 meter" used in songs of mourning. The other two poems, however, are laments in form: ch. 3 an individual lament and ch. 5 a community lament.

In this connection mention should also be made of The Book of Job, a wisdom writing. Although the prose introduction and conclusion to this book portray a pious man who patiently suffered "the slings and arrows of outrageous fortune," the poetic sections depict a figure who, in language even stronger than that of Jeremiah, lashes out against God, protests his innocence, and cries out for vindication.

As has been noted, laments far outnumber any other kind of songs in the Psalter. It is striking that the laments found in Jeremiah's confessions, The Book of Job, and Lamentations have the same general form as the laments found in the Psalter. This suggests that these writers were following an accepted literary convention, as poets frequently do in our Western culture. The form was not confined to Israelite society but was known throughout the ancient Near East. Israel's psalms of lament display a formal resemblance to the songs of its neighbors, especially the Babylonians and the Assyrians. This may be seen, for instance, from the magnificent "Prayer of Lamentation to Ishtar" which comes from the neo-Babylonian period (approximately the time of Jeremiah). It begins with a long ascription of praise to Ishtar, the Queen of Heaven, "who guides mankind aright" and who "regards the oppressed and mistreated." The second movement of the prayer is a lament in affliction to "the goddess of goddesses." Notice the cry "How long?" and the protest of innocence, two typical elements of a lament.

> Let the favor of thine eyes be upon me.
> With thy bright features look faithfully upon me.
> Drive away the evil spells of my body (and) let me see thy
>   bright light.
>
> How long, O my Lady, shall my adversaries be looking upon
>   me,
> In lying and untruth shall they plan evil against me,
> Shall my pursuers and those who exult over me rage against
>   me?

How long, O my Lady, shall the crippled and weak seek me
    out?
One has made for me long sackcloth; thus I have appeared
    before thee.
The weak have become strong; but I am weak.
I toss about like flood-water, which an evil wind makes violent.
My heart is flying; it keeps fluttering like a bird of heaven.
I mourn like a dove night and day.
I am beaten down, and so I weep bitterly.
With "Oh" and "Alas" my spirit is distressed.

I—what have I done, O my god and my goddess?
Like one who does not fear my god and my goddess I am
    treated;
While sickness, headache, loss, and destruction are provided
    for me;
So are fixed upon me terror, disdain, and fullness of wrath,
Anger, choler, and indignation of gods and men.

After pleading faithful devotion to Ishtar, the suppliant
cries out for vindication.

Accept the abasement of my countenance; hear my prayers.
Faithfully look upon me and accept my supplication.
How long, O my Lady, wilt thou be angered so that thy face is
    turned away?
How long, O my Lady, wilt thou be infuriated so that thy
    spirit is enraged?

Turn thy neck which thou hast set against me; set thy face
    [toward] good favor.
Like the water of the opening up of a canal let thy emotions be
    released.
My foes like the ground let me trample;
Subdue my haters and cause them to crouch down under me.

Let my prayers and my supplications come to thee.
Let thy great mercy be upon me.
Let those who see me in the street magnify thy name.[2]

A NET 383

Notice the structural elements of this Babylonian psalm:

Address of praise
Complaint in distress
Protest of innocence
Petition for deliverance
Concluding vow to praise the Deity

This general structure, as we shall see, corresponds closely to Israelite psalms of lament. In fact, we may assume that this cultic form, mediated through the Canaanites, influenced Israelite worship very early, perhaps during the two centuries before David (1200-1000 B.C.) when Israel was occupying the land.

There are, however, profound differences in content. The observation that the Ishtar psalm is polytheistic, while Israelite psalms are addressed to the one God, is true enough but does not go to the heart of the matter. The Babylonian psalm was to be accompanied by a ritual of incantation, that is, a magical spell over the evil spirits (demons). Thus prayer was tied up with magic —the release of a power believed to be effective in overcoming evil. People found themselves in a capricious situation, in which they were not sure what wrong had been done and not certain whether the deity could really deliver them from evil. They were apprehensive in the face of hostile powers that make life precarious. By contrast, the Israelite psalms of lament express the conviction that Yahweh is trustworthy and faithful. The God of Israel has displayed *ḥesed* (covenant loyalty) decisively in the saving experience of the exodus and has come to the aid of the people in the subsequent crises of their history. Unlike human beings who fail to be true to their word, Yahweh's word can be trusted; and Yahweh's word is laden with the power to accomplish its saving purpose.

For as the heavens are higher than the earth,
so are my ways higher than your ways
    and my thoughts than your thoughts;
and as the rain and the snow come down from heaven
and do not return until they have watered the earth,
    making it blossom and bear fruit,
    and give seed for sowing and bread to eat,
so shall the word which comes from my mouth prevail;
    it shall not return to me fruitless
without accomplishing my purpose
    or succeeding in the task I gave it.
                                        —Isaiah 55:9-11 (NEB)

Therefore it is unnecessary to use magic to assist or cajole God to rescue people from distress.

Nevertheless, the People of God finds itself again and again in the interim between God's promise and the fulfillment of the promise. That interim is the time when faith is put to the test; for there are no unambiguous proofs that God has spoken and that God is in control of the human situation. This is the problem with which God's people wrestle throughout the Old Testament period—and beyond. The hymns found among the writings of the Qumran monastery (the Dead Sea scriptures), which flourished at the beginning of the Christian era, contain the same notes of lament, the same motif of "the wilderness of isolation."[3] The New Testament, of course, proclaims that God has spoken decisively in Jesus Christ, thereby endorsing the promises made to Israel. But the Christian community also finds itself living in the interim between the inauguration of God's kingdom and its final realization, between the first break of dawn and the full light of day. Therefore it too knows the trials of faith that are poignantly expressed in the laments of the Psalter. It is reported that Jesus himself uttered the words of one of the laments as a cry of dereliction from the cross: "My God, why hast thou forsaken me?" (Ps. 22:1; see Matt. 27:46 and Mark 15:34); and he died with the words of another lament on his lips: "Into thy hand I commit my spirit" (Ps. 31:5; see Luke 23:46). Thus, Israel's laments were drawn into the context of the passion story and thereby into the history of the People of God which received a new beginning in Jesus Christ.

THE SITUATION OF THE LAMENT

The first thing to notice about the laments in the Psalter is that they fall into two general groups: laments of the community and laments of the individual. The boundary between the two is uncertain, for sometimes, as in Psalm 129, Israel speaks in the first personal pronoun; and at other times, as in Psalm 77, the individual identifies with the affliction of Israel and laments for and with the community. Nevertheless, the following outlines of these two groups of psalms will be useful. Those psalms marked with an asterisk deserve special attention.

COMMUNITY LAMENTS

  *12 "On every side the wicked prowl"
  *44 "For thy sake we are slain all the day long"
   58 "Surely there is a God who judges on earth"
   60 "Thou hast made thy people suffer hard things"
   74 "O God, why dost thou cast us off for ever?"
   79 "The heathen have come into thy inheritance"
  *80 "The bread of tears"
   83 "O God, do not keep silence"
  *85 "That glory may dwell in our land"
   89: "Wilt thou hide thyself for ever?"
38-51 [A royal lament. The first part, vs. 1-37, is a
       hymn]

*90 "Teach us to number our days"
*94 "How long shall the wicked exult?"
123 "We have had more than enough"
126 "Those who sow in tears"
129 "Sorely have they afflicted me from my youth"
137 "On the willows we hung our harps"

(See also the community lament in Lam. 5.)
Captions are from the RSV.

All these psalms express the distress of the community
in a time of threat when people found it difficult to believe
that "God is with us," a fundamental conviction of faith
expressed pregnantly in the word Immanuel ("God with
us," Isa. 7:14; Matt. 1:22-23).

One psalm, Psalm 137, clearly reflects the time of the
Babylonian exile (587-538 B.C.)

> **By the rivers of Babylon we sat down and wept,**
> **when we remembered Zion.**
> **On the willows in that place we hung our harps,**
> **for there those who exiled us demanded of us songs,**
> **and our captors entertainment;**
> **"Sing us some songs of Zion!"**
> **How can we sing the song of Yahweh in a foreign land?**
> **—Psalm 137:1-4**

For the most part, however, the community laments are
lacking in references to concrete historical situations. The
language is so general that psalms of this type could be
used on various occasions, especially the cultic "fast" held
in a time of crisis. Various passages in the Old Testament
allude to times of community mourning and soul-search-
ing (e.g., Judges 20:26; I Kings 21:9-12; II Chron. 20:3-19).

The prophecy of Joel, delivered at a time when a locust
plague threatened the land, reflects one "situation in life"

of the community lament. The country was threatened by an invasion of locusts, likened to an irresistibly advancing army. At one point the prophetic message seems to presuppose a liturgy, consisting of a call to worship, the people's lament and petition to Yahweh, and the "oracle of salvation" which assures worshipers that their prayer has been heard.

A. Call to Repentance (Joel 2:12-16)

> "But now, now—it is Yahweh who speaks—
>   come back to me with all your heart,
>   fasting, weeping, mourning."
> Let your hearts be broken,
>   not your garments torn,
> turn to Yahweh your God again,
>   for he is all tenderness and compassion,
>   slow to anger, rich in graciousness,
>   and ready to relent.
>   —Joel 2:12-13 (JB)

B. Summons to Prepare for a Fast (Joel 2:15-16)
All members of the community, even nursing infants, are to take part in the ceremony.

C. The People's Lament (Joel 2:17)
Standing in the courtyard outside the Temple, between the entrance hall and the altar of burnt offering, the ministers of Yahweh are to lament on behalf of the people:

> Spare your people, Yahweh!
> Do not make your heritage a thing of shame,
>   a byword for the nations.
> Why should it be said among the nations,
>   "Where is their God?"
>   —Joel 2:17b (JB)

D. The Oracle of Salvation (Joel 2:19-27)
God's gracious answer to the prayer comes in the form of "words of assurance," including abatement of the plague.

INDIVIDUAL LAMENTS

More numerous are the individual laments. Originally these laments were composed by persons who, in a time of need or anxiety, went to the Temple to pray. Consider, for instance, the case of Hannah. Having had no child, she went to the temple, once located at Shiloh, and in "great anxiety and vexation" poured out her heart to Yahweh. In this cultic situation the priest, Eli, spoke "words of assurance" to her: "Go in peace, and the God of Israel grant your petition which you have made to him" (I Sam. 1:3-20). We may assume that many of the psalms of individual lament presuppose a setting in worship something like this, though in the course of time they lost their cultic association and became only forms of literary composition. The superscription to Psalm 102, one of "the penitential psalms," is an appropriate introduction to all these laments: "A prayer of one afflicted, when he is faint and pours out his complaint before Yahweh."

*3	"Many are rising against me"	
*4	"In peace I will both lie down and sleep" [Song of trust?]	
5	"Their throat is an open sepulchre"	
7	"Save me from my pursuers!" [Prayer of one unjustly accused]	
9-10	"Why dost thou hide thyself in time of trouble?" [In part a song of thanksgiving]	
✓*13	"Wilt thou forget me for ever?"	
14	"The fool" [Same as Ps. 53]	

70 "Be pleased, O God, to deliver me!"
   [Almost the same as Ps. 40:13-17]
*71 "Upon thee I have leaned from my birth"
*77 "I am so troubled that I cannot speak"
86 "In the day of my trouble I call on thee"
88 "Afflicted and close to death"
89:
38-51 "Wilt thou hide thyself forever"
109 "They reward me evil for good"
120 "Those who hate peace"
*139 "Whither shall I flee from thy presence?"
   [The classification is uncertain. Some regard it
      as the lament of an accused person. Is it a
      hymn?]
140 "By the wayside they have set snares for me"
141 "Let my prayer be counted as incense"
142 "When my spirit is faint"

(See also the individual lament in Lam. 3.)

Captions are from the RSV. The so-called penitential psalms, most of which are individual laments, are listed subsequently (p. 93).

THE FORM OF THE LAMENT

The term "lament" is not an altogether satisfactory label for these psalms. The word may suggest a pessimistic view of life, a "bemoaning of a tragedy which cannot be reversed."[4] But this is not the mood of the psalmists. What characterizes these psalms, with very few exceptions (perhaps Ps. 88), is the confidence that the situation can be changed if Yahweh wills to intervene. Perhaps we should distinguish between a "lamentation" and a "lament." "The lamentation," says Roland Murphy, "is an expression of grief over a calamity that is not reversible [i.e., a dirge], whereas the lament is an appeal to God's compassion to intervene and change a desperate situation."[5] In any case, the psalmists are not like Greek tragedians who portray a no-exit situation of fate or necessity; rather, they raise a cry out of the depths in the confidence that God has the power to lift a person out of the "miry bog" and to set one's feet upon a rock (Ps. 40:1-3). Hence the laments are really expressions of praise—praise offered in a minor key in the confidence that Yahweh is faithful and in anticipation of a new lease on life.

Here we can do little more than delineate the form of the lament in the hope that this will provide a basis for the reader to study the psalms personally, especially those psalms marked with an asterisk in the lists above. In the case of the lament, Israel, as we have observed, borrowed a cultic form known in the ancient world and poured into it the content of its faith in Yahweh. While subject to variation according to the interests and creativity of the author, the form exhibits a definite structure.

A. Address to God
    Sometimes this is a brief cry, though it may be expanded into an ascription of praise (Ps. 9:1-2) or the recollection of God's deeds of old (Ps. 44:1-8).

B. Complaint
    1. In community laments the distress may be military crisis, drought, famine, scourge (cf. I Kings 8:33-40); in individual laments the problem may be sickness, threat of enemies, fear of death, etc. In penitential psalms, the distress is awareness of sin (Ps. 38:4, 18).
    2. Often the complaint is accompanied by a protestation of innocence (Ps. 17:3-5) or a plea for forgiveness.

C. Confession of Trust
This is an expression of confidence in God in spite of the problematic situation; often it is introduced by an adversative such as "but" or "nevertheless" (e.g., Ps. 3:3-6).

D. Petition
The psalmist appeals to God to intervene and deliver, sometimes adducing grounds to support the appeal (e.g., Ps. 6:4-5).

E. Words of Assurance
The suppliant's trust in God finds expression in the certainty that the prayer will be heard. In some laments we deduce that "words of assurance" (an "oracle of salvation") were actually spoken by a priest or prophet (e.g., Ps. 12:5), thus preparing the way for the concluding vow of praise.

F. Vow of Praise
In the confidence that God hears and answers, the suppliant vows to call upon the name of Yahweh and to testify before the community what Yahweh has done (Ps. 7:17; 13:6). In cases where the lament includes "words of assurance," the psalm ends with exclamations of praise (Ps. 6:8-10).

The structure of a psalm of lament is exhibited in the following translation and arrangement of Psalm 22. This prayer, along with Psalm 69 (another lament), is frequently drawn upon in the New Testament for the portrayal of Jesus' passion (see Appendix C). Notice the alternating notes of distress and trust, the repetition of key words and motifs, and the movement from lament to praise.

I. Complaint and Trust

    A. *Cry of Distress*

        My God, my God, why have you   1
            forsaken me?
        and are distant from my cry for
            help, my groaning words?
        O my God, I call out by day, and you   2
            don't answer,
        by night and find no repose.

        Expression of Trust

        But you are holy,   3
            enthroned on the praises of Israel.
        In you our ancestors trusted,   4
            they trusted and you rescued them.
        To you they cried, and they were   5
            delivered;
            in you they trusted and were not
            disconcerted.

    B. *Lament*

        But I am a mere worm, not a person,   6
            disgraced by human beings, scorned
            by people.
        All who see me ridicule me,   7
            they grimace at me and shake their
            heads, [saying]
            "He relied on Yahweh: let him   8
            deliver him!
            Let him rescue him, since he
            likes him!"

Prayer of Confidence

Yet you are the One who drew me out of   9
    the womb,
  who gave me security at my
    mother's breast.
Upon you was I cast from birth,   10
  from my mother's womb you have
    been my God.

II.   Petition out of Distress

Petition for Help

Don't be distant from me,   11
  for I'm in trouble.
Be near!
  for there is no one to help.

A.   *Lament*

Many bulls surround me,   12
  mighty bulls of Bashan encircle
    me.
Open-mouthed to swallow me   13
  are ravenous and roaring lions.
I am drained away like water,   14
  and all my bones are out of
    joint.
My heart has become like wax,
  it melts inside me.
My palate [?] is dry like earthenware,   15
  and my tongue sticks to the roof of
    my mouth.
You have brought me to the point of
    death.

B. *Lament*

> Indeed, dogs surround me,   16
> > a company of evildoers encompass me,
> > they have pierced [?] my hands and feet.
> I count all my bones,   17
> > they gaze at me and gloat.
> They divide my garments among themselves,   18
> > and cast lots for my clothes.

C. *Petition for Help*

> But you, O Yahweh, do not be distant!   19
> > O my Strength, hurry to my aid!
> Rescue my life from the sword,   20
> > my solitary self from the power of the dog!
> Save me from the mouth of the lion,   21
> > from the horns of the wild ox!
> > *You have answered me!**

> [Transition to next section]

III. Praise (Thanksgiving)

A. *Song of Thanksgiving*

> I will proclaim your name to my comrades,   22
> > in the midst of the community I will praise you:

---

*This is a literal translation of the Hebrew. The enigmatic words, which are often emended, may be a transition to the next section, based on words of assurance that the petitioner's prayer has been heard. This is the interpretation of H.-J. Kraus in his commentary on the Psalms.

(Hymn)

"You who fear Yahweh, praise him! 23
　　All you descendants of Jacob, glorify
　　　him!
　　All you offspring of Israel, be in awe
　　　of him!
For he has not spurned or disdained 24
　　the affliction of an afflicted person.
He has not hidden his face from him,
　　but when he cried for help, he
　　　heard."

You are the source of my praise in the
　　great community; 25
　　I will fulfill my vows before those
　　　who fear him.
Let humble ones eat and be satisfied! 26
　　Let those who seek Yahweh praise
　　　him,
their hearts ever full of vitality.

B.　*Renewed Thanksgiving*

Let all the ends of the earth remember 27
　　and turn to Yahweh;
Let all the families of the nations bow
　　down before him!
　　For dominion belongs to Yahweh, 28
　　and he rules over the nations.
　　　　　　　　　　—Psalm 22:1-28**

This pattern, fully elaborated in Psalm 22, is found on a
smaller scale in the beautiful lament in Psalm 13. Notice
that the latter poem moves from a fourfold cry, "How

**The remaining verses, vs. 29-31, are not included in this translation. The
Hebrew text is uncertain at points, but the psalmist continues on a note of
praise.

long?" (vs. 1-2), through a petition for deliverance from the enemy (vs. 3-4), to a concluding expression of trust in Yahweh's covenant faithfulness.

As can be seen from the overall pattern, these cries out of the depths of distress are motivated by a deep confidence that Yahweh is the compassionate God—the God who hears, who is concerned, and who is involved with the people. The God whom Israel worships is not characterized by apathy, but by *pathos*—by sensitivity to the human condition, as Abraham Heschel observed.[6] The scriptural paradigm for this divine sensitivity was given in the Mosaic tradition, and particularly in the story of the burning bush (Ex. 3:7-8), as we have seen (Chapter 2). Given this theological orientation, the movement of the lament is from sorrow to rejoicing, from humiliation to exaltation, and thus toward the song of thanksgiving to be considered in the next chapter.

[Some of the psalms of the Psalter are essentially elaborations of a motif found in a lament. For instance, the protestation of innocence is prominent in some psalms (Ps. 7; 17; 26), and the cry for vindication in others (Ps. 69; 109). In still others, as we shall see presently, the laments are deepened into penitential prayers. And the songs of trust (see Chapter 7) are essentially expansions of the confession of trust which is an essential part of the lament.]

THE PROBLEM OF THE "ENEMIES" IN THE PSALMS

One of the thorniest problems in the psalms of lament is the fact that "enemies" have a central place in prayer to God. This issue also appears in other types of psalms—even psalms of trust such as the Shepherd's Psalm (Ps. 23) which expresses the confidence that Yahweh prepares a table "in the presence of my enemies" (Ps. 23:5). Who are these enemies anyway?

In the case of the community laments, the question is not hard to answer. Laments of this type were used on fast days when the community was threatened by military foes, famine, drought, or some pestilence such as a locust plague (cf. The Book of Joel). Solomon's prayer in the Temple gives a clear picture of the kinds of threat to the people which occasioned community laments (I Kings 8:33-40). In the individual laments, however, we can never be sure what the trouble is, for the psalmists resort to picturesque language to describe the human condition. We have seen this in Psalm 22, quoted above. The psalmist finds himself encompassed by "mighty bulls of Bashan" (v. 12); he feels "drained away like water" and his heart melts like wax (v. 14); he is brought "to the point of death" (v. 15). In shifting imagery he declares that he is attacked by dogs, lions, wild oxen, the sword (vs. 16-21). It is hard to tell from this language whether the suppliant is suffering from sickness, anxiety over death, personal attack by ungodly people, or some other distress.

In one of the most poignant laments of the Psalter, whose theme is "thirst for God," the problem is clearly ridicule and attack by unidentified enemies. From a literary point of view, Psalms 42 and 43 should be regarded as one poem. As we have noticed earlier (Chapter 1), chapter divisions were not found in the original texts but were inserted much later, sometimes arbitrarily. The unity of the poem is evident from the thrice-repeated refrain in which the poet, as in Psalm 103, addresses the whole being—the *nefesh*, or "self."

Why are you so downcast, O my being?
Why do you groan within me?
Put your hope in Yahweh,*
for I will praise him yet,
my personal savior and my God.
                    —Psalm 42:5; 42:11; 43:5

---

*In this psalm, which opens the Elohistic Psalter (Ps. 42-83), editors have substituted the general name for deity (Elohim) for the personal name Yahweh.

[The word "soul" is not used in this translation, for it suggests the ancient Greek view, still influential today, of a deathless entity imprisoned in the body. The Hebrew word *nefesh* refers to the self as a psychosomatic unity.]

Through the psalm breathes the spirit of a close I-Thou relationship and an intense longing for personal communion with Yahweh. It was written in a time of spiritual "dryness" when the poet longed passionately, with the whole being, for Yahweh "the living God"—like a thirsty deer that sniffs for water (Ps. 42:1-2). But this is not a longing for a one-to-one relationship with God in mystic solitude. The poet yearns to be involved in the believing and worshiping community: to participate in the worship services of the Temple and to celebrate with the people the presence of God in their midst. This is not the kind of private piety or spiritual individualism that is often evident today.

Read, preferably aloud, the three stanzas and their respective refrains.

A. In the first strophe (Ps. 42:1-4 + v. 5) the poet portrays a time of "the eclipse of God." Some interpreters suggest that the life situation was sickness that made it impossible to go to the Temple to "behold the face of God," though this is not certain from the text. In any case, this person was exposed to doubts that were aggravated by enemies who raised the incessant taunt: "Where is your God?" The refrain expresses the confidence of one who waits for the eclipse to end and who expects to fulfill a vow of thanksgiving in the Temple.

B. The second strophe (Ps. 42:6-10 + v. 11) plumbs an even deeper level of distress. The poet is far from the Temple—somewhere in the foothills of Mt. Hermon at the source of the Jordan River. But in poetic imagination the tumbling waters of the Jordan fade into the mythical waters of chaos whose "waves" and "billows" pull one downward into the region of death (see Jonah 2:2-9 and the discussion of death, Chapter 4). This spiritual crisis occasions an anguished cry in the presence of faceless enemies who expose the poet's faith to ridicule and doubt.

C. In the final strophe (Ps. 43:1-4 + v. 5) the psalmist's prayer moves to petition for vindication before taunting and oppressing enemies.

Judge [vindicate] me, Yahweh, and defend my case
against untrusting people!
From those who are treacherous and perverse,
rescue me!
For you are the God who defends me—
why have you rejected me?
Why must I go about mournfully
because of the oppression of the enemy?
—Psalm 43:1-2

As in other psalms of lament, the poet anticipates being delivered and presenting a vow of thanksgiving. The prayer is that "light" and "truth," personalized as Yahweh's escorts, will come to guide the suppliant to the Temple to join with the worshiping community in praising Yahweh in music and song.

Various attempts have been made to identify the enemies in the psalms. It has been suggested, for instance, that the laments presuppose a situation of party strife within the Israelite community, like that which broke out in the Maccabean period between the orthodox Jews and those who favored the Greeks. Another proposal is that some of these laments are "prayers of the accused" offered at the Temple, where fugitives found asylum from the hasty, arbitrary justice of pursuers. Psalms 7; 26; 35; 57; 59; and perhaps others (Ps. 139?), suggest this cultic situation.[7] In the presence of the highest Judge, accused persons raised their cry for help, protested their innocence, threw themselves confidently on the mercy of the divine court, and, when a favorable divine verdict was given, raised their voices in thanksgiving. Another suggestion is that the "evildoers" were magicians who, by casting a magic spell, inflicted sickness or calamity upon hapless victims. There are still places in the world where people fear the expert in black magic, witchcraft, or sorcery.

> **His mouth is filled with cursing and deceit and oppression;**
> **under his tongue are mischief and iniquity.**
> **He sits in ambush in the villages;**
> **in hiding places he murders the innocent.**
> **—Psalm 10:7-8 (RSV)**

None of these interpretations is completely satisfactory. The plain truth is that we really do not know who the enemies were, for the psalmists express their distress in stylized language that had been employed for centuries in cultic situations. Indeed, it is striking that the Babylonian psalms of lament used the same conventional imagery (engulfing billows of the flood, miring into the waters of a swamp, descent into the pit, attack by wild beasts, etc.) and even left a blank to be filled in with the name of the worshiper who chose to use the psalm![8] This explains why the enemies in the individual laments are so faceless, and it also helps to account for the fact that these psalms are usable by many different people in times of trouble. The psalmists do not talk boringly about the details of private life, like the proverbial person who inflicts the story of an operation on friends. Nor do they turn introspectively to their own inner life. Rather, by using conventional language they portray a situation that is *typical* of every person who struggles with the meaning of life in the concrete situations of tension, hostility, and conflict. That is why these psalms have been used down through the centuries by suppliants who cry to God out of their concrete situation. They seem to leave a blank, as it were, for the insertion of one's own personal name.

THE CRY FOR VINDICATION

More problematical is the fact that these psalmists—like the prophet Jeremiah in his laments (see especially Jer. 20:7-13)—cry out to God for vindication and even pray for vengeance against the enemies, whoever they are. A number of these psalms are often called "imprecatory" or "cursing" psalms (Ps. 35; 59; 69; 70; 109; 137; 140; and in the category of community laments Ps. 12; 58; 83 strike the same note). Two of these psalms—Psalm 69 and especially Psalm 109—are almost impossible to use in Christian worship. It is often said that the language of these psalms is sub-Christian, that it is out of place in "the new age" governed by the commandment of the Sermon on the Mount, "Love your enemies and pray for those who persecute you" (Matt. 5:44). For many people the magnificent 139th Psalm is ruined by the thought expressed in vs. 19-22 ("Do I not hate them that hate thee, O Yahweh? . . . I hate them with perfect hatred").

The most conspicuous example of imprecation is the closing passage of Psalm 137, a folk song that cried out for vengeance against the Babylonians who destroyed the nation Judah in 587 B.C. and the Edomites who assisted them in the sack of Jerusalem (cf. Obadiah 10-14).

Yahweh, remember
what the Sons of Edom did
on the day of Jerusalem,
how they said,
    "Down with her!
    Raze her to the ground!"

Destructive Daughter of Babel,
a blessing on the man who treats you
as you have treated us,
a blessing on him who takes and dashes
your babies against the rock!
—Psalm 137:7-9 (JB)

It is surely legitimate to question whether the whole Psalter should be retained in Christian worship, including these troublesome passages, or whether the Psalter should be censored at those points which seem to be inconsistent with God's revelation in Jesus Christ. It would be interesting to check the responsive readings included in modern hymnals or books of worship, to see the degree to which the psalms have been edited for Christian worship. Before this question is answered too quickly, however, the voice of contemporary theologians should be heard. Dietrich Bonhoeffer advocated the daily use, especially in our morning and evening devotions, of *all* the psalms. It was his view that we should not "pick and choose," for "otherwise we dishonor God by presuming to know better than he what we should pray."[9] Similarly Christoph Barth objects to the "impropriety" of omitting certain passages that offend us (e.g., Ps. 104:35 or Ps. 139:19-22) and insists: "It is impossible to have the Psalter without its reference to the godless enemies."[10]

It can readily be admitted that the laments of the Psalter are raised from the depths of human anxiety, from which the emotions of bitterness and hatred often well up. The Psalter, like the Old Testament as a whole, is "of the earth, earthy." All the moods and passions of human life find expression here. The psalms do not point to a transhistorical world of pure ideals—the good, the true, and the beautiful; rather, they are concerned with the historical scene of change, struggle, and suffering where God meets people and lays a claim upon them. Psalm 137, quoted above, comes out of a situation of historical struggle where a small people found itself overwhelmed by the massed might of an empire and was suddenly deprived of everything held precious. The Christian community cannot automatically join in this psalm. Yet we must remind ourselves that Psalm 137 has found many parallels in modern life—for instance, during World War II when the pride of France was violated by Hitler's armies, or when brave little Finland was overrun by Russian forces. The question is whether these all too human cries have a place in our speech to God.

We have noticed that the laments use a stylized language that was capable of being reinterpreted in the ever-new situations in which the worshiping community found itself. In describing the enemies in this traditional language, with its monotonous and exaggerated epithets, the psalmists were not calling for a personal fight; rather, they were concerned about the adversaries of the cause of God (as in Ps. 139:19-22). Indeed, there is a strong tendency to associate the enemies with the mythical powers of chaos who stand in opposition to the Creator's purpose. This helps us to understand why the psalmists think of the enemies ("the wicked," "the godless," "the workers of evil") as God's enemies who, as such, are to be hated. "The imagery being mythological," writes Helmer Ringgren, "the enemies are taken to be more than human; they become the representatives of all evil forces that threaten life and order in the world"—the order which the Creator continues to uphold against all the threatening powers of chaos.[11]

The Gospels of the New Testament portray human distress as arising from the threat of demonic powers, organized—according to the apocalyptic view—into an oppressive empire under the rule of Satan. According to this imaginative way of thinking, the human problem is not just the frustration that arises out of one's personal life. Rather, individuals experience the threat of evil powers that are external to them, that affect them in the society in which they live, and that may seduce and overwhelm them, in a time of testing (temptation). Jesus taught his disciples to pray, "Lead us not into temptation, but deliver us from evil," or as the New English Bible translates, "Do not bring us to the test, but save us from the evil one" (Matt. 6:13). We can understand the intention of this language in our time when people, perhaps more than in any other period of human history, find themselves to be victims of structures of power, of antagonisms or prejudices embodied in social customs and behavior, of tremendous social forces or "isms" before which the individual feels helpless. Thus, in the last century, the laments of Negro spirituals expressed "one continual cry"[12] against oppressive pharaohs, and more recently a similar sense of frustration has found expression in the folk songs of young "prophets with guitars." The psalmists' cry for vindication may be closer to our lives than we realize. Oppressed people cry out for justice in the social structures of human society—a justice that would somehow give social expression to love and concern.

THE VENGEANCE THAT IS GOD'S

In trying to answer the questions raised by "the psalms of vengeance" we must keep several things in mind. First, it is important to consider how biblical language is used, that is, the syntax within which words such as "avenge" and "vengeance" function. It is too bad that these words are translated from the Hebrew by English words which in our thought world have a negative connotation. No one wants to be regarded as "vengeful" and therefore it hardly seems right to apply the term to God! However, the Hebrew verb *naqam* ("vindicate") has the basic meaning of "save" in the Old Testament, as it had in other ancient literature, and therefore can be used in exactly the same sense as the Hebrew verb *yashaʻ* ("save") from which the noun "salvation" comes. The language presupposes the view that God has entered into covenant relation with the people Israel, and within the terms of that relationship acts as Judge or Vindicator to defend and uphold justice. Therefore Yahweh's subjects, within the bond of the covenant, appeal to the Suzerain for help, vindication, "salvation." When considered in this light, it is understandable that "*naqam* [to vindicate] is the sole prerogative of God."[13] And this is precisely what we read in the New Testament:

> *Beloved, never avenge yourselves, but leave it to the wrath of God; for it is written, "Vengeance is mine, I will repay, says the Lord."*
>
> —*Romans 12:19 (RSV)*

Here the apostle Paul echoes the note struck in the so-called Song of Moses (Deut. 32:35; see also Heb. 10:30).

In view of this, it is doubtful whether these psalms should be regarded as "imprecatory" psalms or curses in the strict sense. In the ancient world, as in some undeveloped societies today, it was believed that the word spoken in curse released a power, or spell, which was automatically effective. Remember the story in Numbers 22-24 about the diviner Balaam, whom Balak, the king of Moab, employed to destroy Israel with the power of the curse. As long as one believed in the power of "verbal vengeance," prayer was unnecessary.

> *The distinctiveness of the curse lies in the fact that it is aimed directly, without any detour via God, at the one it is meant to hit. A curse is a word of power which the swearer released without recourse to God.*[14]

The Psalter, it is true, contains traces of ancient curse formulas (e.g., Ps. 58:6-9) which probably were dependent upon traditional language used in cultic ceremonies of covenant renewal; but no longer are they curses in the proper sense. They are prayers to God, who obtains vindication in God's own way and in God's own time.

Another thing to consider is that the Old Testament psalms wrestle with the problems of human existence within the context of this life—the "threescore years and ten" of Psalm 90:10. Lacking the eschatological horizon of the New Testament, they concentrate on the problems of life *now* with a fierce and passionate intensity. The psalmists are not satisfied with the notion that the imbalances of life will somehow be corrected in another form of existence beyond historical experience. They believe that God's dealings with human beings take place in this earthly sphere. For them, as for many modern people, death is the final limitation; accordingly, the answers to the pressing questions of human life must be found now. Like a deer that pines for fresh water, they "thirst for God" (see Ps. 42:1 for this figure of speech) with the whole being, and they seek the satisfaction of that thirst in the historical arena, where they live and move and have their being.

In the New Testament the human situation is changed. There the good news rings out that in Jesus Christ, God has conquered the power of death and has thrown open the door into the future. But this victory is only a foretaste of the final consummation when God's action as Judge (Vindicator) will take place. Thus the parable about the unrighteous judge, to whom a widow came persistently with the plea, "Vindicate me against my adversary," ends with the interpretation:

> And will not God vindicate his elect, who cry to him day and night? Will he delay long over them? I tell you, he will vindicate them speedily. Nevertheless, when the Son of man comes, will he find faith on earth?
>
> —Luke 18:7-8 (RSV)

The Christian community reads the psalmists' cries for vindication in the larger context of the biblical story that reaches its climax with the gospel of God's triumph over all the powers of sin, death, and darkness. Already, according to the witness of the New Testament, God the Vindicator has responded to people's anxieties, frustrations, and distresses. Jesus, God's Messiah, has experienced the human cry "out of the depths," as evidenced in the cry of dereliction from the cross (Mark 15:34 quoting Ps. 22:1). But Jesus' death, crowned with divine vindication in the resurrection, enables people of faith to become "more than conquerors" (Rom. 8:31-39) and thus to move from lament to thanksgiving, from death to life.

PSALMS OF PENITENCE

According to a liturgical tradition that reaches back into the Middle Ages, seven psalms are placed under the rubric of penitential psalms. This classification, however, is based on content rather than on literary form, for one of them is actually an individual song of thanksgiving (Ps. 32, Augustine's favorite psalm). In these instances the affliction from which suppliants plead for deliverance is a deep sense of guilt. Each psalm deserves your special attention.

PENITENTIAL PSALMS

*6	"My soul is sorely troubled"
*32	"Thou didst forgive the guilt of my sin"
	[Song of thanksgiving]
*38	"There is no health in my bones because of my sin"
*51	"Create in me a clean heart, O God"
*102	"I mingle tears with my drink"
*130	"Out of the depths I cry to thee"
*143	"Enter not into judgment with thy servant"

Captions are from the RSV.

Sometimes, as in Psalm 143, these psalms refer to "enemies"—external powers that oppress and crush a person. However, these laments are different from others considered previously in that they internalize the problem of evil. The enemy is not just "out there" in society but is also present "here" in the depths of one's own being. In these psalms the presence of the Holy God in the midst of the people is experienced as both inescapable judgment (see Psalm 139 again!) and gracious acceptance. It might be helpful to approach these psalms by reading the account of the prophet Isaiah's experience in the Temple (Isa. 6). Isaiah's vision of Yahweh's holy, transcendent majesty prompted a cry of distress:

> *Woe is me! I am shattered!*
> *For a man of unclean lips am I,*
> *and in the midst of a people of unclean lips I am living.*
> *For the King, Yahweh of Hosts, my eyes have seen.*
>   *—Isaiah 6:5*

According to the account, which is still echoed in the familiar hymn "Holy, Holy, Holy," the prophet came to realize that divine holiness is manifest, not just in judgment that exposes human sin but in forgiveness that purifies and empowers for a task (cf. Ps. 130:4).

Miserere

The cry *Miserere* ("Have mercy"), which resounds through the music and liturgy of Christian tradition, is the opening exclamation of Psalm 51, one of the pearls of the Psalter. This psalm is found in the so-called Elohistic Psalter, a section in which the personal name of Yahweh was replaced by Elohim (God). Undoubtedly the poet originally used the personal form of address, appealing to Yahweh's abounding *ḥesed* (covenant faithfulness) as in other liturgical contexts (Ps. 103:6-7; 136; cf. Ex. 34:6-7).

Notice that the structure of this exquisite poem corresponds to that of the lament outlined above (see pp. 76-77).

A. Address (Ps. 51:1-2)
A cry for deliverance from sin, based not on any human merit or achievement but solely on Yahweh's grace and faithfulness.

B. Complaint (Ps. 51:3-5)
A profound and inescapable awareness of guilt before Yahweh: "Against you, you only, have I sinned."

C. Petition (Ps. 51:6-12)
In a series of imperatives, the suppliant pleads with Yahweh to act: "purge me," "fill me," "create in me," "restore me."

D. Vow of Praise (Ps. 51:13-17)
The suppliant concludes by promising to bear witness in the worshiping community to Yahweh's re-creating grace.

Clearly the person who composed this psalm was not a slavish devotee of the liturgy of the Temple or, as we might say, the forms of organized religion. As a token of gratitude for deliverance from guilt ("the bondage of sin"), we are told, the only appropriate and acceptable sacrifice to God is "a broken and contrite heart." Like the classical prophets of Israel (e.g., Isa. 1:10-17), the psalmist was critical of the Temple services, especially the sacrifices that were presented (see Lev. 1-7). The psalmist's language, in fact, was so sharply critical that a later revisionist added a qualification at the end of the psalm (vs. 18-19), thereby justifying the use of the psalm in Temple services. Yet in spite of this criticism, the psalmist was profoundly dependent on the forms of worship, as indicated by references to ritual washing (v. 2) and to purification with hyssop (v. 7)—an aromatic bush used in rites of cleansing (Lev. 14:4; Num. 19:18). The forms of worship, according to this psalmist, signify nothing unless they are outward expressions of an inward relationship to God.

There is one statement in this psalm which presents a special theological difficulty:

> **Behold, I was brought forth in iniquity,**
> **and in sin did my mother conceive me.**
> **—Psalm 51:5 (RSV)**

In the past this sentence has been taken to mean that sex is inherently sinful, though necessary for procreation, and that sin is transferred genetically from one generation to another. This dubious understanding of "original sin" finds no support here. The poet is speaking existentially—not proposing a "doctrine" that applies to human beings generally. From the standpoint of the existing self, the poet looks back over his life to its very beginning in his mother's womb and confesses that the whole story of his life stands under Yahweh's scrutinizing judgment. No attempt is made to exonerate himself by laying the blame on heredity or environment: the problem lies in his own being—a self that exists in broken relationship to God and a self that can be renewed only through a new act of creation:

> **Create in me a clean heart, O God,**
> **and put a new and right spirit within me.**
> **Cast me not away from thy presence.**
> **and take not thy holy Spirit from me.**
> **—Psalm 51:10-11 (RSV)**

Here the special verb *bara'* ("create"), a verb that is used only of an action that God performs freely (Gen. 1:1; Isa. 45:12; etc.), describes divine action that restores the self to a faithful relationship.

[The Hebrew word for "heart," which is here parallel to "spirit," does not refer to the seat of the emotions as in English (in Hebrew that would be "kidneys" or "bowels"). Rather, "heart" refers to the mind and the will, that is, the center of the self from which action and loyalty spring.]

De Profundis

Another penitential psalm that deserves special attention is Psalm 130, in liturgical tradition designated by the opening Latin words *De Profundis* ("Out of the depths"). Here again we find the main elements of a lament:

A. Initial appeal to Yahweh (Ps. 130:1-2)
B. Portrayal of inward distress (Ps. 130:3-4)
C. Expression of confidence (Ps. 130:5-6)
D. Witness of praise to the community (Ps. 130:7-8)

Since the title of this book is based on the opening words of this psalm, a special word of comment is appropriate. In the poet's speech, the word "depths" reverberates with the mythical overtones of the abyss of watery chaos, the realm of the powers of confusion, darkness, and death that are arrayed against the sovereign power of God. To be drawn into the realm of chaos (the sphere of death) is to be separated from the world in which people praise God and find fulfillment in the worshiping community (see discussion of death, Chapter 4). In this instance, however, the poet uses the mythical language to speak about separation from God that results from human freedom (sin). Indeed, the distance between the Holy God and sinful humanity is so infinitely vast that if God were to keep account of iniquities, no one would have a leg to stand on (v. 3).

The key sentences of the psalm are found toward the beginning:

Yahweh, if you kept track of sins,
Lord, could anyone stand?
But with you there is forgiveness,
so that you may be revered.
—Psalm 130:3-4

The psalmist goes on to say that it is this forgiving word for which one waits and hopes, like watchmen who wait through the long night hours for the dawn (v. 5). But why should God's forgiveness arouse "reverence" (the Hebrew word means "fear")? Some may find this a strange, if not jarring, note in the psalm. The declaration, however, is consistent with the psalmist's sense of the holiness of God, before whose searching judgment no one can stand with an easy conscience. Divine forgiveness is not "cheap grace," as might be inferred from the jest of the dying poet Heinrich Heine, that "it is God's business to forgive." God's forgiveness is not something that comes necessarily or naturally. It is wrong to say that God forgives *because* that is what is expected of God or *because* something in the human situation merits it. Forgiveness is the expression of God's grace, of God's freedom to "be gracious to whom I will be gracious" and to "show mercy upon whom I will show mercy" (Ex. 33:19; see Rom. 9:15). God's forgiveness, then, is a wonderful gift, the appropriate response to which is wonder and praise.

THE PARADOX OF RIGHTEOUSNESS

The penitential psalms, taken as a whole, seem to stand out from, and even conflict with, other psalms in the Psalter.

They agree on the fact that there is no human ground for *claiming* God's grace *(ḥesed)*. Indeed, in one of these psalms it is said that if Yahweh were to enter into judgment with a person, the case would be hopeless from the outset.

Do not put your servant on trial,
for no living being is righteous before you!
—Psalm 143:2

In the presence of God there is human equality because of the democracy of sin. High and low, rich and poor, wise and ignorant come together at the altar. The only ground for human appeal is the "righteousness" and the "faithfulness" of God (Ps. 51:1; 143:1; etc.).

In contrast stand laments that are based on the "righteousness" of the suppliant. How are we to understand these? For instance, one lament contains the appeal:

Judge [vindicate] me, Yahweh, according to my
righteousness,
according to the integrity that is in me.
—Psalm 7:9; also Ps. 26:1

Moreover, some laments, following traditional literary form (see above, pp. 76-77), include protestations of innocence, as in the psalm just quoted (vs. 3-5). Indeed, in some instances this element is emphasized (e.g., Ps. 17:3-5; 26:4-7; 18:20-24; 59:3-4). We are reminded of Job, who, before he was overwhelmed by the voice out of the whirlwind, protested that he was innocent and that his record was essentially clean (Job 31). In the end, of course, Job came to realize that his vaunted innocence was no ground for judging God, the Creator whose ways transcend human comprehension.

Admittedly, we are now facing a theological problem that is difficult to resolve, especially in view of the fact that strict consistency cannot be expected in a book of worship that was composed over a long period of time and includes many theological voices. Nevertheless, the question ought to be explored as to whether the psalms of "innocence" are in absolute conflict with the psalms of "penitence." As Dietrich Bonhoeffer remarked, "The notion that we can never suffer innocently so long as within us there still hides some kind of defect is a thoroughly unbiblical and demoralizing thought."[15] In facing this question we should divest ourselves of notions of righteousness that we have inherited from our culture, largely under Greek and Roman influence. Normally we assume that a "righteous" person is one who conforms to some legal or moral standard. Such a person is held to be righteous according to the law ("law" here being interpreted in terms of Greek *nomos* or Roman *lex*). Stated in other terms, people measure themselves, or others, by whether they live up to certain ideals or a particular code of behavior. See the caricatured portrayal of the Pharisee in the New Testament parable (Luke 18:9-14).

Another view of righteousness is illustrated in the story found in Genesis 15:1-6. In a lament (v. 2) Abraham complained that he (and the People of God) could not possibly have a future when he was without a son and the only legal heir was his household servant. How could God be true to the promise made earlier (Gen.12:1-3; 13:1-17), when, humanly speaking, there was no possibility of fulfillment? The story goes that Abraham was led outside his tent, where he could view the heavens. With no other evidence than the myriads of stars in the sky, Abraham was assured that his descendants would be myriad. Then comes a crucial sentence:

> *Abram put his faith in Yahweh,*
> *who counted this as making him justified.*
> —Gen. 15:6 (JB)

This story illustrates what it means to be "righteous" (or "justified," according to the above translation) in the sight of God (see Gen. 6:9). Clearly Abraham's righteousness was not the achievement of moral perfection; that can hardly be said in view of the story in Genesis 12:10-20 which tells how his self-interest put his wife in jeopardy! Rather, the righteousness accounted to him was *being in right relationship* with God, as shown by his trust in God's promise even when there was no evidence to support it—none but the myriads of stars in the sky! What made Abraham a whole person, a man of integrity, in the judgment of God was his loyal and trusting relationship, not the incidents that demonstrated that he was prone to error and subject to human weakness.

The passage in Genesis 15 asserts that righteousness (right relationship) was "accorded," "reckoned," or "granted" as a divine verdict. The Hebrew idiom seems to reflect a cultic situation in which God deems a person to be "righteous," that is, to be in a loyal, trustful relationship. It may be that the psalms of righteousness (innocence) also reflect a situation in the Temple, where this approval was granted to suppliants. In any case, righteousness in this theological sense is a gift of grace, not a human achievement.

This view of righteousness, as something that one does not assert but is *given*, dominates the New Testament, especially the writings of the apostle Paul. Righteousness (justification), according to Paul, is not something that a person achieves, but is a free gift that God grants to faithful persons through Jesus Christ. Therefore Paul stands before God "not having a righteousness of my own, based on law, but that which is through faith" (Phil. 3:9). In this view, Christians experience in their own way what members of the Israelite community experienced in worship: the divine recognition of "righteousness" or the right relationship of trust and dependence upon God, which amounts to "salvation." The alternative attitude toward God was expressed by the "wicked," "the fools" who supposed they could live out of their own resources, as though God were not to be reckoned with.

Righteousness, then, does not mean being without defect in the presence of God. If that were the case, the so-called psalms of penitence could not be prayed by the worshiping community. The strange thing is that it is the "righteous," "the pious," "the faithful," "the innocent" who pray the so-called penitential psalms. For it is only when people stand in a right relationship with God—that is, having a righteousness which they cannot claim as a prerogative but which is graciously granted them in the relationship of the covenant—that they can assert their innocence and plead for God's forgiveness. "It is the righteous who confess their unrighteousness before God," writes Christoph Barth; "only the godless man refuses to do this, because he regards himself as righteous." We are left, then, with the apparent paradox of "the righteousness of the sinner."[16]

EXPOSTULATION WITH GOD

All the laments in the Psalter, whether community or individual laments, are cries out of the depths of human suffering. Even the so-called penitential psalms belong together essentially with the other laments in this respect, for in them bodily sickness and spiritual affliction are inseparably fused, as in the New Testament stories of Jesus' miracles.

Instil some joy and gladness into me,
  let the bones you have crushed rejoice again.
Hide your face from my sins,
  wipe out all my guilt.
          —Psalm 51:8-9 (JB); cf. Ps. 32:3-5

What characterizes all the laments, however, is that suffering is not accepted patiently or stoically; instead, people dare to expostulate with God with a faith that seeks understanding. Through all of them, with passionate intensity, reverberates the poignant outcry, "Why?" Claus Westermann's remarks about the laments of the community Israel apply also to individual laments:

> How can God bring such profound suffering upon his people—if indeed they are his people—when he has previously done such great things for them? Insofar as the absurd is laid before God, the lament of the nation contains a dimension of protest, the protest of a people who cannot understand what has happened or has been done to them. It is protest directed at God, to be sure, but it is nevertheless protest; it does not endure absurdity submissively and patiently: it protests.[17]

These protests, however, are all based on one grand conviction: the God who is supremely worthy of worship, and to whom people cry out even in the time of "the eclipse of God," is the faithful God, the God of hesed. That basic premise of trust, which is found in all the psalms of lament, releases people to expostulate with God, as was the case with Abraham (Gen. 18:22-33), Moses (Ex. 32:7-14), Jeremiah (Jer. 15:15-18), Job, and other heroes of faith. In the psalms of lament, then, we do not find people shaking their fists in protest at a cold and brassy heaven or resigning themselves grimly to impersonal fate, but people who testify, even in times when they walk through the valley of dark shadow, that God is faithful and concerned and therefore hears their cry. It would be a mistake to overemphasize the element of petition in the psalms of lament and to disregard the element of trust.

Laments, then, are praises in the time of God's absence, when God's "face" (presence) is hidden. These poignant human outcries express a faith that dares to question and even to wrestle with God in situations of suffering and distress. Perhaps there is something therapeutic in prayer of this kind.[18] It is a trait of human nature to want the simple answers, the packaged doctrines, the secure orthodoxy; but the psalmists display the kind of faith that is honest to God and that boldly seeks for the meaning and purpose of life.

Perhaps people today are coming to know, even more radically than the psalmists, that this is a time of "waiting for God," a time of hope for some new manifestation of God's presence in human experience. The modern awareness of the absence of God is not irrelevant to worship; it may become the occasion for prayer of lament "out of the depths."

NOTES

1. Claus Westermann, *The Praise of God in the Psalms,* 2d ed., tr. Keith R. Crim (John Knox Press, 1965), p. 37.

2. Translated by Ferris J. Stephens in James B. Pritchard (ed.), *Ancient Near Eastern Texts Relating to the Old Testament,* 3d ed. (Princeton University Press, 1969), pp. 383-385.

3. Theodor H. Gaster, *The Dead Sea Scriptures in English Translation* (Doubleday & Co., Anchor Books, 1956), p. 112. Gaster objects to the prosaic interpretation of the enemies in these psalms ("the company of Belial," "the men of corruption") as adversaries escaped or overcome in warfare. Such a view, he remarks, "confuses the 'sling and arrows of outrageous fortune' with concrete bazookas and guided missiles."

4. In a study of "Jeremiah's Complaints" (*Journal of Biblical Literature,* Vol. 82 [1963], p. 50n.), Erhard Gerstenberger proposes that instead of "lament," which "bemoans a tragedy which cannot be reversed," we use the word "complaint," which implores God to reverse the situation. But the word "complaint" has difficulties too. Claus Westermann suggests that we make a distinction between "the lament of affliction" and "the lament of the dead." "The lament of the dead," he writes, "looks backward, the lament of affliction looks forward." ("The Role of the Lament in the Theology of the Old Testament," *Interpretation,* Vol. 28 [1974], p. 22.)

5. Roland E. Murphy, *The Psalms, Job,* Proclamation Commentaries (Fortress Press, 1977), pp. 16-17, 41 (quotation).

6. Abraham J. Heschel, *The Prophets* (Harper & Row, 1965), esp. Chs. 12-18.

7. This view has been advanced by Hans Schmidt, *Die Psalmen,* Handbuch zum Alten Testament, 15 (Tübingen: J. C. B. Mohr, 1934).

8. Helmer Ringgren's brief discussion of "The Psalms and Comparative Religion," in *The Faith of the Psalmists* (Fortress Press, 1963), pp. 115-21, is helpful in this connection.

9. Dietrich Bonhoeffer, *Psalms: The Prayer Book of the Bible,* trans. J. A. Burtness (Augsburg Publishing House, 1970). Bonhoeffer's view is discussed by John D. Godsey in *The Theology of Dietrich Bonhoeffer* (Westminster Press, 1960), p. 191.

10. Christoph Barth, *Introduction to the Psalms,* trans. R. A. Wilson (Charles Scribner's Sons, 1966).

11. Ringgren, *The Faith of the Psalmists,* p. 45; see also pp. 44-46. This theme is discussed in Bernhard W. Anderson, *Creation Versus Chaos* (Association Press, 1967), Ch. 5, "Creation and Conflict."

12. This phrase is quoted by James H. Smylie in his article, "On Jesus, Pharaoh, and the Chosen People: Martin Luther King as Biblical Interpreter and Humanist," *Interpretation,* Vol. 24 (1970), p. 78.

13. G. Ernest Wright, "Reflections Concerning Old Testament Theology," in *Studia Biblica et Semitica,* ed. Theodorus C. Vriezen (Wangeningen, The Netherlands: H. Veeman & Zonen, 1966), p. 387.

14. Claus Westermann, *A Thousand Years and a Day* (Fortress Press, 1962). See also Helmer Ringgren, *The Faith of the Psalmists,* pp. 31-32.

15. Dietrich Bonhoeffer, according to Godsey, in *The Theology of Dietrich Bonhoeffer,* p. 193.

16. Christoph Barth, *Introduction to the Psalms,* p. 42.

17. Westermann, "The Role of the Lament," p. 30.

18. For a discussion of the meaning of psalms of lament for pastoral counseling, see Donald Capps, *Biblical Approaches to Pastoral Counseling* (Westminster Press, 1981), Ch. 2.

4
SINGING
A NEW SONG

Orientation toward the future was characteristic of Israel's faith from the very first. Unlike the Canaanites, whose religion tended to bind people to particular places, Israel was summoned to go with Yahweh into the future—like a flock that follows its shepherd into unexplored trails and new pastures, to recall the imagery of the well-known Twenty-third Psalm. In the Old Testament we do not find a nostalgia for the past or, still less, a settling down in the present, but a movement toward the future.

This movement from the past through the present to the future is portrayed dynamically in the psalms of lament that we considered in the last chapter. In psalms of this type, poets remember the past—"the faith of our fathers and mothers" and the wonderful demonstrations to them of God's saving power. This retrospective view, however, only heightens the spiritual problem of the present, when in the time of "the eclipse of God" children find it difficult, if not impossible, to live by the faith of their parents. Hence, a keynote of psalms of lament is "waiting for God."

Wait for Yahweh!
Be strong and courageous in your heart!
Yes, wait for Yahweh!
—Psalm 27:1

This waiting, however, does not have the ambiguity portrayed in Samuel Beckett's play *Waiting for Godot*. The psalmists wait for the God known by the personal name Yahweh, whose presence in history was manifest in the past and whose presence would be revealed again on the horizon of the future. In these contexts, the verb "wait" expresses a straining toward the future, a keen anticipation of what is to come. Hope is waiting with one's whole being for the dawn when the re-creating word of forgiveness will be spoken (Ps. 130:5-6); it is waiting eagerly for Yahweh the King to come with saving power (Isa. 40:10-11, 30-31). Thus the psalms of lament move "From Hurt to Joy, From Death to Life" (Walter Brueggemann).[1]

When the righteous cry, Yahweh hears,
  and rescues them from all their troubles.
Yahweh is near to the brokenhearted,
  and saves those who are crushed in spirit.
                   —Psalm 34:17-18

SONGS OF THANKSGIVING

The alphabetical acrostic Psalm 34, just quoted, is usually classified as a song of thanksgiving. Before we consider the form and content of this type of psalm, a word should be said about its relationship to the lament, on the one hand, and to the hymn of praise on the other.

The lament almost invariably moves from the minor mode of complaint or penitence to the major key of thanksgiving and praise (see Chapter 3). In the certainty of being heard by God, the suppliant—whether the community or the individual—looks forward to God's deliverance from a situation of limitation or distress; and, in anticipation of God's gracious action, the lament ends with a vow of praise (Ps. 7:17; 13:6; 22:22-31; 56:12-13;

etc.). Thus the lament in Psalm 57 concludes with a song of thanksgiving:

My heart is resolved, O Yahweh,*
  my heart is resolved.
I will sing and play!
Awake, mine honor [self],
  Awake, O lute and harp!
I will awake the dawn!
I will praise [thank] you among the peoples, Lord,
  I will play tunes to you among the nations.
For great toward the heavens is your faithfulness,
  and your fidelity reaches to the skies.
In the heavens be exalted, O Yahweh,*
  on the earth may your glory be known!

—Psalm 57:7-11

This "abrupt change of mood" in the laments, to which Hermann Gunkel once called attention, is quite striking. It is doubtful whether it can be explained solely on the basis of the psalmist's inner certainty. It seems likely that the transition from sorrow to rejoicing, from lament to thanksgiving, was occasioned by something that occurred in the setting of worship within which these psalms had their place. There is reason to believe that at a certain moment in the service a member of the Temple personnel, a priest or sometimes a prophet, pronounced an "oracle of salvation" which assured the suppliant of God's grace and favor. None of these "oracles" has been preserved, but now and then we find hints that they were spoken. For instance, at one point in the community lament, Psalm 85, apparently a minister listens for, and summarizes, an "oracle of salvation."

---

*Here editors have substituted the general name for deity (Elohim) for the personal name of address, Yahweh. This psalm belongs to the Elohistic Psalter (Ps. 42-83).

Let me hear what God, Yahweh, speaks,
  for he proclaims welfare [peace] to his people,
  to his loyal devotees. . . .
Truly his salvation is near to those who fear him,
  so that glory may dwell in our land.
                                    —Psalm 85:8-9

Possibly indications of priestly oracles are also found in
such passages as Psalms 12:5; 55:22; 91:14-16; 121:3-5.

Thus it was the "word of God," mediated through the
service of worship, that modulated the tone of a
suppliant's prayer from lament to rejoicing. We may
assume that in Psalm 28, for instance, at the conclusion of
the lament (vs. 1-5), a minister of the cult delivered words
of assurance, to which the suppliant then responded in
grateful praise:

Blessed be Yahweh,
  for he has heard my cry for favor!
Yahweh is my strength and my shield,
  in him my heart trusts.
So I am supported and my heart exults,
  and with my song I gratefully praise him.
                                    —Psalm 28:6-7

This cultic situation reminds one of Christian services of
worship in which the liturgical sequence is: confession of
sin and need, "words of assurance" or absolution, and
then a doxology or other act of praise.

It can be seen, then, that a very close relationship exists
between the lament and the thanksgiving. Indeed, the
"song of thanksgiving" is an expanded form of the
thanksgiving already present in many of the laments (Ps.
6; 13; 22; 28; 31; 55; 69; 71; 86; etc.). However, it is one thing
to praise God *in anticipation* of deliverance or on the basis
of an assurance given in worship; it is another thing to

praise God *in response* to an event of deliverance already experienced. It is the latter accent which characterizes the songs of thanksgiving. These songs are sung by people who, after a time of patient waiting (Ps. 27:13-14: a lament), have experienced the goodness of God in the everyday world.

> **Taste and see how good Yahweh is!**
> **Happy is the one who finds refuge in him!**
> **—Psalm 34:8**

Looking in another direction, we see that the songs of thanksgiving are also closely related to hymns of praise (see Chapter 5). The English reader is apt to think that all psalms which begin with an invocation to "give thanks" to God must be thanksgivings. But this is not necessarily so, for the Hebrew verb *hodah* cannot be limited to the meaning of our word "to thank"; it has the wider connotation of "acknowledge," "confess," "proclaim," and therefore is often used in parallel with verbs meaning "praise," as in the hymn:

> **Enter his gates with thanksgiving,**
> **and his courts with praise!**
> **Give thanks to him, bless his name!**
> **—Psalm 100:4 (RSV)**

Therefore we are really dealing with two ways of praising God, which can be distinguished from each other only by the form and content of the psalm. In one case, the psalmist praises God in general terms, extolling the God whose Name is majestic in heaven and earth, whose sovereign might rules human history (e.g., Ps. 8; 33). This is the hymn. In the other case, the psalmist praises God for particular action in a concrete situation of limitation and distress. This specific praise is what we mean by the song of thanksgiving. It must be admitted, however, that sometimes the line between the hymn and the song of thanksgiving cannot be drawn sharply. For instance, the beautiful prayer found in Psalm 103 (to be considered later) is sometimes regarded as a song of thanksgiving and sometimes is classified as a hymn. And Psalm 100, a hymn, is labeled "A Psalm for the thank offering [todah]" in the superscription.

The songs of thanksgiving, like the laments, may be divided into songs of the community and songs of the individual, though sometimes this division is uncertain, since the first personal pronoun "I" may be used in both.

The community songs of thanksgiving are relatively few in number, and even these come close to being hymns. Perhaps the reason for this is that in corporate praise, which transcends the situation of individuals, the community tends to use the form of the hymn that extols God's saving power in broader terms: the mighty acts of God in history or the display of God's providential care in creation. In any case, the community songs of thanksgiving were used in the major festivals at the Temple, especially the great fall harvest festival of ingathering (see Chapter 6).

COMMUNITY SONGS OF THANKSGIVING

 65 "Thou crownest the year with thy bounty"
     [This may be regarded as a hymn]
 67 "The earth has yielded its increase"
 75 "We recount thy wondrous deeds"
     [Classification uncertain; possibly a liturgy]
*107 "Let them tell of his deeds in songs of joy!"
*124 "The snare is broken and we have escaped!"
136 "His steadfast love endures forever!"
     [This litany may be regarded as a hymn]

(See also the community thanksgiving in I Sam. 2:1-10.)

Captions are from the RSV.

The individual songs of thanksgiving, on the other hand, were composed for recitation at the Temple as an expression of a person's praise to God for deliverance from a concrete distress, such as illness. In that cultic situation the individual "acknowledges" or "testifies" (the meaning of the Hebrew verb *hodah*) that Yahweh has acted in his or her situation in life. Since the word usually translated "thanksgiving" *(todah)* is the same word used for "thank offering" (Jonah 2:9; Ps. 50:14, 23), it is clear that these psalms were intended to be used in a cultic setting, that is, at a festival or other worship service at the Temple. On such an occasion the individual, in the presence of the worshiping congregation (Ps. 22:22; 26:12b), testified personally to God's saving deeds to the accompaniment of a ritual act (a thank offering). This is the picture given in a passage in Jeremiah which announces that in the time of restoration the voices of mirth and gladness will be heard once again, including "the voices of those who sing, as they bring thank offerings *[todah]* to the house of Yahweh":

> *Give thanks [testify] to Yahweh of hosts,*
>   *for Yahweh is good,*
>   *for his faithfulness endures for ever!*
>   —*Jeremiah 33:11*

In this manner the individual confesses out of personal experience the faith of the whole believing community whose shared history is a witness to Yahweh's saving deeds.

INDIVIDUAL SONGS OF THANKSGIVING

18   "With the loyal thou dost show thyself loyal"
       [A royal thanksgiving]
21   "In thy strength the king rejoices"
       [A royal thanksgiving, paired with Ps. 20: prayer for the king's victory]

30   "Thou hast turned my mourning into dancing"
*32   "Thou dost encompass me with deliverance"
       [One of the penitential psalms]
*34   "Look to him, and be radiant!"
       [This alphabetic acrostic is possibly a wisdom
          psalm]
40:    "He put a new song in my mouth"
1-11   [The second part of the psalm is a lament]
66:    "I will tell what God has done for me"
13-20 [The first part of the psalm is a hymn]
*92   "At the work of thy hands I sing for joy"
*103   "Your youth is renewed like the eagle's"
       [Probably to be classified as a hymn]
108   "Awake, O harp and lyre!"
       [A mixed type: composed of Ps. 57:7-11
          (thanksgiving) and Ps. 60:5-12 (lament)]
*116   "I will lift up the cup of salvation"
*118   "This is the day which the LORD has made"
       [A liturgy of royal thanksgiving]
*138   "On the day I called, thou didst answer me"

(See also the individual songs of thanksgiving in Isa.
38:9-20 and Jonah 2:2-9)

Captions are from the RSV.

Notice that in the above list three of the psalms are
designated as royal thanksgivings. In these the king ("the
anointed one"—in Hebrew, the word equivalent to
"messiah") speaks not just as an individual but as the
representative of the people. This is the case in Psalm 118
(Luther's favorite psalm)—a psalm that is often quoted in
the New Testament. (See Appendix C.) The king's song of
thanksgiving in vs. 5-21 is offered in a cultic situation, as
evidenced by the request for admission through the
Temple gates so that he may give thanks (v. 19), the
choral blessing from the Temple (v. 26), and the solemn

festal procession to the altar (v. 27). Thus the worshiping community takes part in the thanksgiving and identifies itself with the king's testimony to the saving power of God. It is not surprising that a psalm which belonged so deeply to Israel's worship was eventually referred to *the* Anointed One (Messiah), as happens in the New Testament. In the larger context of the Christian Bible the central image of this psalm—the stone, rejected by the builders, which has become the chief cornerstone (vs. 22-25)—is identified with Jesus Christ, the "king," whom God has exalted from rejection and humiliation to a crucial place of honor in the divine purpose (Matt. 21:42; Acts 4:11; I Peter 2:7). And since in every Christian worship service the community celebrates God's triumph in Christ with praise and thanks, it is appropriate for the liturgist to say on "the Lord's Day" (Sunday, the day of resurrection):

This is the day which the Lord has made;
let us rejoice and be glad in it!
—Psalm 118:24 (RSV)

THE STRUCTURE OF THE SONG OF THANKSGIVING

The song of thanksgiving is cast in a form which, allowing for variations, may be traced quite clearly in the songs of the individual.

A. Introduction
   Some indication is given of the worshiper's intention to give thanks to God. The opening invocation, which may be short or omitted altogether, is usually made to Yahweh in the second person ("thou"), as in Psalm 30, for example.

B. Main Section: Narration of the Psalmist's Experience
   1. Portrayal of the distress that the suppliant once experienced
   2. The suppliant's cry for help
   3. The deliverance

C. Conclusion
   The worshiper again testifies to Yahweh's gracious act. A prayer for future help, or a confession that Yahweh is gracious, or some other formulation may be added.

As an example to guide in the study of the psalms marked with an asterisk in the above list, let us consider the psalm of thanksgiving that has been inserted into the story of Jonah. We say "inserted" because the psalm is obviously out of place in its present context. In the belly of a "fish" a cry for help (i.e., a lament) would be appropriate, but not a thanksgiving for deliverance already experienced!

A. Introduction: A summary of the Testimony of the Psalmist (Jonah 2:2)

   Recollection: Distress

   Out of my distress I cried to Yahweh,
   *   and he answered me;*
   from the belly of Sheol I cried,
   *   and you have heard my voice.*

B. Main Section
   1. Portrayal of Affliction (Jonah 2:3-6a)

   You cast me into the abyss,
   *   into the heart of the seas,*
   *   and the flood encompassed me.*

All your waves, your billows
  overwhelmed me.
Then I thought: I am banished
  from your presence.
How shall I ever again see
  your holy Temple?
The waters engulfed me right to my throat,
  the deep encompassed me.
Seaweed was twisted around my head
  at the bases of the mountains.
I sank down into the underworld
  whose gates were closing me in forever.

2. Cry for Help and Answer (Jonah 2:6b-7)

But you brought me up alive from the Pit,
  Yahweh, my God!
When my life was ebbing away,
  I remembered Yahweh,
and my prayer reached you
  in your holy Temple.

3. Deliverance
(This motif is found at the preface to the petition: "But you brought me up alive from the Pit.")

C. Conclusion: Acknowledgment of God's Gracious Act and Promise to Present a Thank Offering (Jonah 2:8-9)

Those who worship worthless idols
  abandon their [true] loyalty.
But as for me, with a song of thanksgiving [todah]
  I will offer a sacrifice to you.
The vow I have made, I will fulfill.
  Salvation is from Yahweh!

In reading this psalm one is struck with the poetic imagery: the poetic portrayal of the threat of death as sinking down into the subterranean waters of chaos to the depths of Sheol, the realm of death. Later we shall consider the mythopoeic view of the cosmos (portrayed in the artistic sketch, p. 123) and the dynamic view of life and death that is expressed in the poetic idiom: "Deep calls to deep" (as in the lament, Ps. 42:7-8). Here our concern is with literary form, and particularly the difference between a lament and a thanksgiving.

The example from The Book of Jonah shows that a song of thanksgiving looks back to a former time of distress when a suppliant, in a situation of lament, cried to Yahweh for help. That situation, however, no longer prevails. The interim of God's absence, reflected in psalms of lament, has ended. In response to a cry out of the depths, Yahweh has graciously acted. Once again Yahweh has "shown his face" (presence) and this new situation in life calls for the singing of "a new song."

I waited and waited for Yahweh,
  and he turned to me,
  and heard my cry.
He raised me out of the pit of despair,
  out of the miry clay,
and he set my feet on a rock,
  securing my steps.
He has put on my lips a new song,
  praise to our God.
Many will observe and fear,
  and will put their trust in Yahweh.
               —Psalm 40:1-3

It is noteworthy that these songs of thanksgiving retained their basic form even after they were detached from their original cultic setting and became "spiritual songs." This is evidenced in the songs of thanksgiving found among the Dead Sea scriptures, to which we referred previously (Chapter 1). These songs characteristically begin with the testimony, "I thank thee"; then follows an address to the Deity; this in turn is followed by a clause, introduced by the motive word *ki* (usually translated "for," "that"), which gives the specific reason for offering thanks to God.[2] This thanksgiving genre, which was current in the Judaism out of which Christianity emerged, came to be prominent in the New Testament "eucharistic" tradition. ("Eucharist" comes from a Greek verb meaning "to thank.") The epistle to the Ephesians contains this advice to the Christian community:

> *Be filled with the Spirit, addressing one another in psalms and hymns and spiritual songs, singing and making melody to the Lord with all your heart, always and for everything giving thanks in the name of our Lord Jesus Christ to God the Father.*
>
> —*Ephesians 5:18b-20 (RSV)*

Lifting the Cup of Salvation

Psalm 116 is an excellent example of the literary form called the song of thanksgiving.

A. Introduction (Ps. 116:1-2)
    The psalmist begins by ascribing praise to Yahweh and giving the motive *(ki)* for praise.

B. Retrospect (Ps. 116:3-9)
    The poet then recalls the past experience:
    Cry for Help. In a time of distress, when the power of death had almost prevailed, the suppliant appealed to Yahweh for help and Yahweh answered (vs. 3-4).

Motive of Trust. This recollection prompts an expression of trust in Yahweh, the gracious God (vs. 5-7).

Divine Answer. This section concludes with a testimony to the amazing grace that restored the suppliant's being (vs. 8-9).

For you have delivered my life from death,
my eyes from tears,
my feet from stumbling.
I walk before Yahweh in the land of the living.
—**Psalm 116:8-9**

C. Conclusion: Vow of Praise (Ps. 116:10-19)
Finally, in gratitude for Yahweh's gracious action the suppliant lifts a libation in the presence of the worshiping community as a testimony to the divine grace that supports all the people:

What shall I give back to Yahweh
for all his bounty to me?
The cup of salvation I'll lift,
and call on the name of Yahweh.
My vows to Yahweh I will complete
here in the presence of all his people.
—**Psalm 116:12-14**

The picture on page 120 of a votive offering in the form of lifting "the cup of salvation" may be only a metaphor here, but at one time it was a cultic act, on which archaeology has shed some light. Otto Eissfeldt draws our attention to a Phoenician votive stele (upright stone) from the fifth century B.C. belonging to Yehawmilk, king of

A king presenting a libation cup before a goddess

From a Phoenician votive stele, fifth century B.C. See
J. B. Pritchard, *The Ancient Near East in Pictures Relating
to the Old Testament* (No. 377). Illustration after the
original: Joan Anderson. All rights reserved.

Byblos. The text is addressed to the goddess Ba'alat, the female counterpart of the great storm-god Baal:

> Yehawmilk, king of Byblos, to my lady, Ba'alat of Byblos. For when I cried to my lady, Ba'alat of Byblos, then she heard me and showed me favour.

Interestingly, there is a picture above the inscription which shows the king standing before the goddess, who is seated on her throne. In his hand he holds a libation cup, which he lifts up to her. Thus the acknowledgment of thanks and the thank offering are combined in this votive stele, precisely as they are combined in the psalms.[3] Here again we have evidence that Israelite worship was influenced by ancient forms of worship, though these forms were transformed to express Israel's distinctive faith. Indeed, this thanksgiving rite of "lifting the cup" has survived in both Jewish and Christian liturgy. Paul, for instance, refers to "the cup of blessing" in a discussion of the Lord's Supper (I Cor. 10:16).

DELIVERANCE FROM THE POWER OF DEATH

One passage in Psalm 116 deserves special attention. It is the passage in vs. 3-4 which provided the motif for Bach's chorale, "Christ lag in Todesbanden" ("Christ lay in the bonds of death"). Here an affirmative view of life is linked with a realistic view of death.

The cords of death encompassed me,
  the snares of death gripped me,
  distress and anguish came upon me.
Then I called upon the name of Yahweh:
"O Yahweh, please save my life!"
                    —Psalm 116:3-4

The view of life and death presupposed in the psalms is quite different from modern biological conceptions. Most people think of a death as a biological event that occurs when the heart stops beating and consciousness goes out like a light. Death, according to this generally accepted notion, comes *at the end of life*. This terminus is often recognized with a mixture of melancholy and sentimentality in the ritual of the funeral service—especially funerals that are taken out of the context of the worshiping congregation and handed over to the funeral parlor.

The psalms are filled with an awareness of the brevity and frailty of human life (Ps. 90:3-10; 103:14-16). But what strikes us most is the psalmists' view that death works its power in us *now*, during our historical experience. According to the Israelite view, death brings about "a decrease in the vitality of the individual."[4] Death's power is felt in the midst of life to the degree that one experiences any weakening of personal vitality through illness, handicap, imprisonment, attack from enemies, or advancing old age. Any threat to a person's welfare (Hebrew *shalom*, peace, well-being), that is, one's freedom to be and to participate in the covenant community, is understood as an invasion of the empire of death into the historical arena.

This reference to death's imperialism—its territorial ambition to encroach into "the land of the living"—deserves further consideration. The psalmists' portrayals of the threat of death are couched in a pictorial (mythical) language expressive of a way of thinking which, at first glance, seems alien to our experience. Israel inherited a picture of the universe that depicted the world as surrounded on every hand by "the waters of chaos" which, at the time of creation, the Creator subdued and pushed back in order to give creatures space in which to live and to perform their God-given tasks (Gen. 1:1-2:3). The earth is portrayed as a kind of island, suspended over

THE ANCIENT PICTORIAL VIEW OF THE UNIVERSE

1.   The waters above and below the earth
2,3,4.   Chambers of hail, rain, snow
5.   The firmament with its "sluices"
6.   Surface of the earth
7.   Pillars supporting the firmament
8.   The navel of the earth: "fountain of the Great
         Deep"
9.   Sweet waters (rivers, lakes) on which the
         earth floats
10.   Sheol, the realm of Death (the "Pit")

the waters of the "deep," within which is located Sheol, the kingdom of death; and beyond the great blue dome overhead are the waters of the heavenly ocean which, unless held back by the protective barrier of the firmament, would flood the world with chaos (as almost happened, according to the Flood story, Gen. 6-9). It is wrong to convert this pictorial view into a prescientific "three-storied conception of the universe," as has happened in some modern discussions of the Bible. In the psalms this language is used religiously or poetically to express the awareness that on all sides the historical world is threatened by powers of chaos which, were they not held back by the Creator, would engulf the earth and reduce existence to meaningless confusion.

This helps us to understand the many references in the Psalter to coming into deep waters, to the engulfing waves and billows, or to the "descent into hell" (Sheol, the Pit, Abaddon ["the place of destruction"]). In the psalm of Jonah, as we have noticed, the suppliant cries to Yahweh "out of the depths." Using poetic imagery he says that he has been "cast into the deep," that the waves and billows have gone over him, and that he has plunged, like a drowning man, down to the very roots of the mountains. The same imagery is found in the royal thanksgiving, Psalm 18 (see vs. 4-6). In the latter psalm, however, the divine rescue is vividly described in terms of mythical language appropriated from the Canaanites. Yahweh is portrayed as the Divine Warrior who, in an awe-inspiring theophany of thunderstorm (vs. 7-15; cf. Ps. 29:3-9), comes to battle with the waters of chaos (the mythical sea) and drives them back to their place.

He reached from the heights and took me,
he drew me out of mighty waters.
He delivered me from my strong enemy,
and from my adversaries more powerful than I.

In the time of my disaster they accosted me,
but Yahweh became my support.
He brought me out into a spacious place,
he delivered me because he delighted in me.

                    —Psalm 18:16-19

Here we see how the historical enemies of the king are associated with the powers of chaos which threaten God's creation (see also Ps. 144:1-11).[5]

In the Canaanite mythology which has profoundly influenced these portrayals, Death (Mot) was regarded as a god in his own right—the powerful king of the underworld. According to Ugaritic mythological literature from about 1400 B.C., Mot seeks to extend his kingdom over the earth and thereby challenges the authority of 'El, the father of the gods. However, the youthful storm-god, known as Aleyn Baal, takes up the challenge and wins a great victory over Mot, whereupon Baal is acclaimed as king. The conquest of death is not decisive, however; it has to be repeated every year as the cycle of the seasons moves from the barrenness of winter to the renewal of fertility in the spring, from death to resurrection. The Israelite faith, in confrontation with the Baal religion which dominated Canaan, repudiated the view that the meaning of human existence is given in the rhythms of nature. It proclaimed, rather, God's historical actions in decisive, nonrecurring events (chiefly the exodus) which called the people Israel into being and guided them in their historical journey. However, Israel appropriated the old mythical language and reinterpreted it to express historical experiences of threat and limitation which seemed to call into question the sovereignty of God. In the psalms, death is a power (though no longer a deity) that reaches out greedily to lay hold of the living, a deposed king whose shadowy kingdom encroaches upon the historical world, an enemy that stands in opposition to the purpose of God. The psalmists testify that it is only God who can save one from death's power.[6]

In the psalms this struggle against the encroachment of death into the historical world is never resolved by a clear and unambiguous expression of belief in a future life. Indeed, when we read in English translation the affirmation, "Thou hast delivered my soul from death" (Ps. 116:8), we must guard against reading into the word "soul" the notion of an element within the body which by nature is deathless and indestructible. The Greek doctrine of the "immortality" (deathlessness) of the soul is not attested in the Old Testament, or for that matter even in the New Testament. Only God is essentially immortal (I Tim. 6:16); 'adam (human being) is a mortal who, as the story in Genesis 2 puts it, is made "from the ground" and "returns to the ground." The word translated "soul" (Hebrew, nefesh) means "self" or "person" as a psychosomatic unity. If the self has a future, as indeed the New Testament emphatically proclaims, God will—in a marvelous way, past our comprehension—raise it and give it a new "body," a new form of existence. The "resurrection of the body" (i.e., the self) is attested in Paul's great discussion in I Corinthians 15, and of course is basic to the church's creedal affirmation: "I believe in the resurrection of the body [not "flesh"] and the life everlasting." This Christian view, however, is not found in the Psalter, though there may be intimations of a future life here and there (see Chapter 7).

What, then, is the concern of the psalmists when they give thanks to Yahweh for delivering them from the power of death? Certainly they are not just glad to regain physical health, or to add more years to their life, or to enhance the life they now enjoy with greater comfort or security. That is a modern conception of life, whose emptiness is eventually disclosed. According to Israel's way of thinking, life is missed when people do not *choose* it (see Deut. 30:15-20 with its alternative: "See, I have set before you life and death. . . . Therefore choose life!"). Moreover, the life of "the righteous" is eroded in vitality when death works its power. As Christoph Barth observes, what the psalmists pray for in laments, or thank God for in thanksgiving is "the restoration of life that they have lost" or "its radical renewal through true life"—that is, the life that is given through relationship to God in the covenant community.[7] For the psalmists the tragedy of death is that it transposes people into another, nonhistorical realm where they can no longer praise God.

Dost thou work wonders for the dead?
Do the shades rise up to praise thee?
Is thy steadfast love declared in the grave,
or thy faithfulness in Abaddon?
Are thy wonders known in the darkness,
or thy saving help in the land of forgetfulness?
—Psalm 88:10-12 (RSV); also Ps. 6:5

When a person is separated from a community wherein people remember and celebrate the goodness of God, life ebbs to the vanishing point. On the other hand, when a person is restored to a meaningful place in the believing and worshiping community, when one's relationship to God and fellow human beings is renewed, then it is possible for life to begin again and for the person to join in the singing of praises with the whole *nefesh*, or being. The Germans have a nice way of expressing what it means for the individual to be restored to community: *Leben ist loben* ("To live is to praise").

CROWNED WITH LOVE AND MERCY

The theological perspective on life in relationship to God may be seen by turning to Psalm 103, "one of the finest blossoms on the tree of biblical faith" (Artur Weiser). We cannot be certain about the classification of this psalm. Often it is regarded as a "thanksgiving for recovery from sickness" (as in *The Oxford Annotated Bible*, RSV).[8] On the other hand, one could argue that the psalm is a hymn because of its lack of concrete reference to a life situation and its general expression of praise. Probably we have here a song which wells up from an individual's thanksgiving for healing and expands into hymnic praise. In any case, the psalm provides an excellent transition from the thanksgivings considered in this chapter to the hymns of praise to be considered in the next.

The psalm falls into three parts, on the scheme of concentric circles—each dealing with the self, the community, and the cosmos respectively. The starting point (the inner circle) is the life story of an individual and from this point the poet's thought expands to the farthest reaches of the cosmos.

1. In the first part (Ps. 103:3-5), the poem exuberantly discloses that the poet's life story is the sphere of Yahweh's saving activity. Indeed, the *nefesh* (self, being) is addressed as "you" and is summoned to thank Yahweh, who "forgives all *your* iniquities," who "heals all *your* diseases," who "redeems *your* life from the Pit [Sheol]," who "crowns *you* with *ḥesed* and mercy," who revitalizes *you* with a vigor like that of the proverbial eagle. This personal language may indicate that the psalmist's praise arises out of thanksgiving.

2. In the second part (vs. 6-18) the psalmist's thought expands outward to the community with which the psalmist is identified, as evidenced by the grammatical shift from singular pronouns to plural ("us," "our"). The same "amazing grace" (*ḥesed*) has been evident in Israel's history, right back to the beginning when Yahweh "made known his ways to Moses, his acts to the people of Israel" (Ex. 33:12-33; 34:8), by taking the side of the oppressed.

3. In the third part (vs. 19-22) the psalmist's praise ascends above individual and social experience to the cosmos, over which Yahweh is enthroned in transcendent majesty. Every creature in heaven and earth is summoned to join in the anthem which originates in the life of a solitary person. With literary artistry, the psalm is rounded off at the end by returning to the note sounded in the beginning: "Bless Yahweh, my whole being."

Psalm 103 is like a jewel that glistens from various angles. Notice how, in this case, the self is related to the drama of Israel's history. Standing within the community whose tradition reaches back to Moses, an individual testifies out of personal experience to the same divine grace that has supported the people as a whole. In this sense, the psalm is related to the storytelling psalms considered earlier (Chapter 2).

One of the striking aspects of Psalm 103 is that the poet reflects on the motive behind the divine grace that constitutes a covenant people. In the exodus story, to which the poet refers (v. 7), Yahweh's *hesed* is an expression of divine freedom (Ex. 33:19: "I will be gracious unto whom I will be gracious"), and this freedom is manifested in Yahweh's decision to go with the people in spite of their fickle, sinful ways. In this psalm, however, a motive for Yahweh's display of *hesed* is suggested: Yahweh knows our human weakness and our mortal frailty. Therefore, says the psalmist, Yahweh has compassion—like a father who pities his children or, one may add, like a mother who consoles her young (Isa. 66:13).

The days of human beings are like grass,
  like flowers of the field they flourish:
    for a wind blows over them and they vanish,
    and their place does not know them anymore.
But the faithfulness [*hesed*] of Yahweh is endless
  upon those who fear him,

and his righteousness extends to future generations,
to those who keep his covenant,
those who remember his commandments and obey them.
—Psalm 103:15-18

The heart of Israel's faith pulses in the poetry of this psalm. It is God's faithfulness which endows the individual's life, the history of the people, and the whole cosmos with ultimate meaning.

THE OLD TESTAMENT LOVE OF LIFE

A robust this-worldliness characterized Israel's faith. The notion that this world is only a preparation for the next, or that earthly experience is lower and therefore inferior to some higher realm of reality, is completely alien to the Old Testament. This view, which still prevails in much Christian thinking, originated under the influence of Hellenistic philosophies which drew a sharp distinction between the eternal realm of unchanging Reality and the temporal realm of change, flux, and contingency where eternal truth is, at best, only intimated in a shadowy form. The psalms, however, bear witness to the fundamental goodness of life as God has given it to us. All the senses—sight, hearing, taste, touch, and smell—are to be employed in the enjoyment of life to the full, in whatever time is given. To be sure, this love of life is not a shallow sense of happiness such as modern people try to find in the midst of sensual pleasures and technological benefits. There is, as we have noticed repeatedly, a minor strain of grief, anxiety, and even God-forsakenness which runs through life's experiences. But even the sufferings and perplexities of everyday life are transmuted into praise by people of faith who expect to "see the goodness of Yahweh in the land of the living" (Ps. 27:13). This hope is not postponed indefinitely or transferred to an otherworldly existence. The songs of thanksgiving joyfully announce that the saving presence of God is experienced again and again in the everydayness of human life. People of faith celebrate with joy and thanksgiving, knowing that "God's Yes is spoken in the midst of life" (Claus Westermann).

It is therefore highly appropriate that the Christian church, which has heard God's Yes pronounced decisively in Jesus Christ, should find its faith nourished by the psalms of the Old Testament. Dietrich Bonhoeffer, the martyred Christian whose life and thought have profoundly influenced Christian theology in our time, came to appreciate the life-affirming, this-worldly faith of the Old Testament more and more during his career. In an Advent meditation, composed in prison before his death, he wrote:

> *My thoughts and feelings seem to be getting more and more like the Old Testament, and no wonder, I have been reading it much more than the New for the last few months. It is only when one knows the ineffability of the Name of God that one can utter the name of Jesus Christ. It is only when one loves life and the world so much that without them everything would be gone, that one can believe in the resurrection and a new world. It is only when one submits to the law that one can speak of grace, and only when one sees the anger and wrath of God hanging like grim realities over the head of one's enemies that one can know something of what it means to love and forgive them. I don't think it is Christian to want to get to the New Testament too soon and too directly.[9]*

There is much truth in this. Those who bypass the psalms, with their taste for the goodness of life, are apt to miss the fullness of the New Testament gospel which announces that Jesus Christ came that people might have life and have it abundantly (John 10:10).

NOTES

1. Walter Brueggemann, "From Hurt to Joy, From Death to Life," *Interpretation*, Vol. 28 (1974), pp. 3-19.

2. James M. Robinson discusses the genre of the "thanksgiving" and the "blessing," both of which appear prominently in the psalms of Qumran (Dead Sea Scrolls), in his essay in *The Old Testament and Christian Faith*, ed. Bernhard W. Anderson (Herder & Herder, 1969), esp. pp. 131ff.

3. Otto Eissfeldt, *The Old Testament: An Introduction* (Harper & Row, 1965), p. 122. He concludes: "Thus the Phoenician cultus, too, was familiar with the gesture of thanksgiving which the psalm passage attests [Ps. 116:13], and the words quoted from the inscription lead to the surmise that there existed there, too, songs of thanksgiving similar to those of the Old Testament, as we have similar ones in Egypt in fair numbers and in fact from a very early date."

4. See the monograph by Aubrey R. Johnson, *The Vitality of the Individual in the Thought of Ancient Israel* (Cardiff: University of Wales Press, 1949).

5. See further Bernhard W. Anderson, *Creation Versus Chaos* (Association Press, 1967), esp. pp. 93-99.

6. In this connection see the penetrating discussion of "The Power and Overthrow of Death," by Christoph Barth, *Introduction to the Psalms*, trans. R. A. Wilson (Charles Scribner's Sons, 1966), pp. 49-55. See further Lloyd R. Bailey, Sr., *Biblical Perspectives on Death* (Fortress Press, 1979).

7. Christoph Barth, *Introduction to the Psalms*, pp. 50-51, 54-55. In this context he observes: " 'Life' for the psalms means the historical formation and appearance of the people of God, while 'death' means their sinking back into the natural existence of the heathen, fundamentally without history."

8. *The Oxford Annotated Bible*, Revised Standard Version, ed. Herbert G. May and Bruce M. Metzger (Oxford University Press, 1962), p. 734.

9. Dietrich Bonhoeffer, *Prisoner for God: Letters and Papers from Prison* (Macmillan Co., 1953), p. 79. See also Martin Kuske, *The Old Testament as the Book of Christ: An Appraisal of Bonhoeffer's Interpretation*, trans. S. T. Kimbrough, Jr. (Westminster Press, 1976), pp. 96ff.

5
THE WONDER
OF GOD'S CREATION

Israel's praises, as we have seen, were evoked in the first instance not by a general religious awareness of God's wisdom and power manifest in the broad expanse of creation or in the sweep of human history but rather by the experience of Yahweh's saving power and purpose in the life situation of a people. Yahweh's intervention into the historical plight of a band of slaves—victims of the mightiest emperor of the time—had the wonderful effect of creating a people "out of nothing" and opening a way into the future from a no-exit situation. Hence Israel's earliest songs, as in the case of the Song of Miriam (Ex. 15:21) or the Song of the Sea (Ex. 15:1-18), were jubilant cries of praise in response to the God who had acted with saving power.

Since Israel turned primarily to its own historical experience to find the musical themes of praise, it is appropriate that we have considered initially psalms that express prayer to God out of concrete distress (the laments) and the praise to God for a particular act of deliverance just experienced (songs of thanksgiving). However, these songs "out of the depths" inevitably lead in the direction of *hymns* which praise God in general terms: for God's greatness and faithfulness as Creator of the cosmos and Ruler of history. The lament found in Psalm 102, for instance, contains hymnic elements (vs.

12-22, 25-28). And Psalm 107, a thanksgiving on behalf of various groups—those who had traveled safely in the desert, those delivered from prison, those healed from sickness, and those who voyaged safely on storm-tossed ships—appropriately concludes with a hymn of praise for God's providential care (vs. 33-43).

Psalm 98 is an excellent illustration of how life-situational praise of God, the "Vindicator" of Israel, leads to the singing of "a new song" in which all the inhabitants of the earth and even the vast realms of nature are summoned to worship.

Sing Yahweh a new song,
  for he has performed marvels,
his own right hand, his holy arm,
  gives him the power to save.

Yahweh has displayed his power;
  has revealed his righteousness to the nations,
mindful of his love and faithfulness
  to the House of Israel.

The most distant parts of the earth have seen
  the saving power of our God.
Acclaim Yahweh, all the earth,
  burst into shouts of joy!
                              —Psalm 98:1-4 (JB)

In this hymn Israel's horizon expands from the praise of "our God"—the God dynamically present in Israel's historical experience—to general praise of the God who is Creator and Lord of the whole earth.

THE FORM AND SETTING OF THE HYMN

The hymn (Hebrew, *tehillah*) is concisely defined as "the song which extols the glory and greatness of Yahweh as it is revealed in nature and history, and particularly in Israel's history."[1] This definition rightly indicates that Israelite hymns placed particular stress upon Yahweh's active involvement in the life story of Israel. In the so-called storytelling psalms (Chapter 2) the "mighty deeds" of Yahweh were retold didactically "so that the next generation might know them" (Ps. 78:1-8); and during the great festivals Yahweh's actions probably were reenacted in a ritual drama so that worshipers might "see" what God had done for Israel and thereby experience directly the power and meaning of the drama of Israel's history (compare Ps. 66:5, 6; 46:8).[2] But it is equally true that the hymns of Israel have a universal and cosmic dimension. In the Temple of Jerusalem, worshipers confessed that the "glory" or splendor of Yahweh which filled the sanctuary also suffused the whole universe. This is evident from the account of Isaiah's call (Isa. 6) where, in the prophet's vision, the Jerusalem Temple seems to be a miniature of the heavenly temple in which Yahweh is enthroned as *the* King. The hymn that the prophet hears resounding in the heavenly temple is undoubtedly the echo of one that was sung in the earthly sanctuary in Jerusalem:

Holy, holy, holy is the LORD *of hosts;*
the whole earth is full of his glory.
—*Isaiah 6:3 (RSV)*

The structure of the hymn is found in its simplest form in the Song of Miriam (Ex. 15:21 [see Chapter 2, pp. 47-48]), which begins with an imperative summons to praise and continues with an announcement of the motive for praise (introduced by the motive word, *ki*). This form is found also in the shortest psalm of the Psalter, Psalm 117:

A.   **Praise Yahweh, all nations!**
     Extol him, all peoples!

B. For *[ki]* great is his faithfulness toward us,
and the fidelity of Yahweh is unending.

C. Praise Yahweh!

[The concluding hallelu-jah ("Praise Yah[weh]") is sometimes regarded as the beginning of the following Psalm 118, as in the Greek translation of the Old Testament. But such a conclusion is found at the end of Ps. 104; 105; 106; 113; 115; 116. In this case too it is probably a formal part of the psalm. The first verse of the psalm is quoted in Romans 15:11.]

Here is a psalm that is purposefully short and simple, as Luther once remarked, so that anyone can grasp its meaning. The simplicity of the content is matched by the clarity of its form.

As the above outline indicates, the hymn contains the following elements:

A. Introduction: Call to Worship
This is usually an imperative, in the second person plural. It can be a "bidding" formula such as "O come, let us sing" (Ps. 95:1-2) or a summons addressed to the psalmist's *self*, such as "Bless [praise] Yahweh, O my being" (Ps. 104:1). The note struck in the introduction may be repeated in the psalm (e.g., 95:6) or even expanded to great length (as in Ps. 148).

B. Main Section: The Motive for Praise
In many cases the transition to the motive for praise is introduced by "for" (Hebrew, *ki*), as in Ps. 33:4 or 95:3 and 7. This is sometimes varied by using "who" clauses, as in Ps. 104:2ff. or by introducing long passages that portray God's majesty as displayed in history or creation (e.g., Ps. 33:4-19).

C. Recapitulation
   Often the psalm concludes with a renewed summons to praise, thus echoing the note struck at the beginning.

In the genre of the hymn the most important element is the main section, which gives the ground or motive for praise. A typical example is this hymnic outburst in the poetry of Second Isaiah:

> Break into singing together,
>   you ruins of Jerusalem!
> For [ki] Yahweh has comforted his people,
>   has redeemed Jerusalem.
> —Isaiah 52:9

Or again:

> Shout with joy, O heavens,
>   for [ki] Yahweh has acted.
> Raise a shout, you depths of the earth!
> Break into singing, O mountains,
>   you forests with all your trees!
> For [ki] Yahweh has redeemed Jacob,
>   has displayed his glory in Israel.
> —Isaiah 44:23

Hymns with this form were undoubtedly used on a variety of worship occasions in the Temple, much as general hymns of praise in modern hymnbooks are used in regular services of worship. Other hymns seem to have been used for special festal occasions, corresponding to special music used in churches today at Christmas, Thanksgiving, or Easter. A number of hymns, the so-called psalms of Yahweh's enthronement, were probably used in connection with the great festival held in Jerusalem in the autumn (the New Year festival). These "enthronement psalms," along with psalms celebrating the Davidic kingship and the choice of Zion, will be considered in Chapter 6.

In the following outline the hymns of praise are grouped according to three general thematic categories: God's creation (redemption) of Israel; God's creation of the world; and God's sovereignty over history. Admittedly, the assignment of a hymn to a particular theme is somewhat arbitrary, but the arrangement provides a helpful sequence for study. As usual, an asterisk indicates those psalms which deserve special attention.

I. HYMNS TO GOD, WHO CREATED (REDEEMED) ISRAEL

66:	"Come and see what God has done!"
1-12	[The second part of the psalm is an individual song of thanksgiving]
✓*100	"He made us and we are his"
111	"He sent redemption to his people" [An acrostic psalm]
*114	"When Israel went forth from Egypt"
149	"Let Israel be glad in his Maker"

Other hymns outside the Psalter:

*The Song of the Sea	Ex. 15:1-18
The Song of Moses	Deut. 32:1-43
The prayer of Habakkuk	Hab. 3:2-19
Good Tidings of Peace	Isa. 52:7-10

II. HYMNS TO GOD, WHO CREATED THE WORLD

*8	"When I look at thy heavens"
*19:	"The heavens are telling the glory of God"
1-6	[The second part of the psalm is a meditation on the Torah]
95:	"In his hand are the depths of the earth"

1-7a   [Note that vs. 6-7 strike the note heard in psalms
           listed above: the creation of Israel]
*104   "In wisdom thou hast made them all"
*148   "He commanded and they were created"

Other hymnic passages:
           God the Creator and King   Ps. 74:12-17
           [Interlude in a lament]
           The Incomparable God   Ps. 89:5-18
           [Included in a psalm of the Davidic covenant]

III. HYMNS TO THE CREATOR AND THE RULER
       OF HISTORY

 *33   "He spoke and it came to be"
*103   "Your youth is renewed like the eagle's"
 113   "He raises the poor from the dust"
 117   "Extol him, all peoples!"
*145   "The eyes of all look to thee"
           [An acrostic psalm]
*146   "I will sing praises to my God while I have being"
*147   "He sends forth his command to the earth"

(See also the hymns to Yahweh, the King [Ps. 47; 93;
95-99], considered in the next chapter.)

Captions are from the RSV.

   Psalm 150 is not included in the above outline because,
as we have noted previously, it is a doxology which
rounds off the whole Psalter. Nevertheless, it is particularly interesting in this context, because it calls upon a whole
orchestra of instruments, including trumpet, lute, harp,
timbrel, strings, pipe, and cymbals, to join in praising
Yahweh. This psalm clearly indicates that Israel's praise
was not a quiet meditation but rather the making of a
"joyful noise" to Yahweh "with timbrel and dance" (v. 4;
cf. Ps. 33:2-3; 149:3). Such a psalm is reminiscent of the

earliest days when Miriam and her companions praised Yahweh to the accompaniment of "timbrels and dancing" (Ex. 15:20-21). Here again we notice that worship, being the response of the whole being to God's overture, may take the form of bodily movement, set to the rhythms of music and dance. This does not necessarily suggest the frenzied excitement of prophetic groups who used music, drugs, and dancing to stimulate religious ecstasy (cf. I Sam. 10:5-6, 9-13). It is perhaps more like the Greek dramas in which the chorus, through singing and dancing, expressed the people's involvement in the drama.

THE NAME OF GOD

The hymn was not unique with Israel. Thanks to archaeological research we now have at our disposal a large treasury of hymns from Israel's neighbors: hymns to Amon-Re, to Ishtar, to Marduk, and to other gods and goddesses worshiped by Egyptians, Sumerians, Babylonians, Hittites, and Canaanites.[3] What is unique about Israel's hymns is that they are praises of *Yahweh, the God of Israel.* This praise found expression in a new kind of speech to God. In some respects this new speech carried over idioms of the past: for instance, the expression "a great King above all gods" (Ps. 95:3) is traditional language, based on the ancient picture of the King who presides over the heavenly council, "the assembly of the holy ones" (Ps. 89:5-6; cf. I Kings 22:19; Job 1:6). What is more important here is that Israel praised Yahweh by pouring *new content* into the ancient form of the hymn. Israel's hymn is appropriately called "a new song" (Ps. 96:1; 98:1).

In Chapter 1, when introductory matters pertaining to the Psalter were under consideration, we noticed that one collection of psalms stands apart because of its use of the general term for deity, Elohim (God), in preference to the special name Yahweh (Lord). This Elohistic Psalter (Ps. 42-83) was compiled in a circle that was reticent to use the name Yahweh. This reverence in regard to the name is so striking that it focuses attention sharply on the fact that the Psalter as a whole ascribes praise to Yahweh. When Elijah challenged the people at Mt. Carmel, "If Yahweh is God, follow him; but if Baal, then follow him" (I Kings 18:21), none answered; but the answer of the psalmists would have been immediate and clear: "Know that Yahweh is God!" (Ps. 100:3); "Bless Yahweh, O my soul; and all that is within me, bless his holy name!" (Ps. 103:1). Since Israelite faith was at no stage a tolerant polytheism, or even a predilection for one supreme God out of many, the stress upon the divine name deserves attention. Usually Christian worshipers skip lightly over this matter when reciting the words of the Lord's Prayer: "Hallowed be thy name."

In the ancient Israelite world, as in some societies today, the question of the name was a supremely important issue—one that could not have been challenged, as it was in Shakespeare's tragedy, with the innocent query, "What's in a name?" (*Romeo and Juliet*, Act 2, Scene 2). Among the Israelites the name was understood to be the expression of the nature or identity of a person.[4] Although in our society names have tended to become labels, we can still appreciate the Israelite view, at least imaginatively. Nothing is more pathetic than a man who, because of amnesia, cannot remember his own name, that is, who he is. And nothing is more shocking than the report that prisoners in concentration camps were divested of their personal names and given numbers. A person's name designates the self that has a particular history, a unique life story. To be introduced to a person by name, if the introduction leads into any depth of relationship, is to perceive and, to some degree, to enter into the life story of the person who bears the name.

From this standpoint we may begin to understand the Israelite concern to know the name of God. God's personal name symbolizes God's identity, who God is; and God's self-revelation is given in the context of a story, a history. Therefore the God whom Israel worships is identified in "who" clauses which may be a narrative reduced to a single sentence, as in the prologue to the Decalogue: "I am Yahweh, your God, who brought you out of the land of Egypt, out of the house of bondage" (Ex. 20:2). Psalm 136, which has been referred to previously in connection with our discussion of storytelling psalms (Chapter 2), is a long chain of "who" clauses, punctuated with the antiphonal refrain:

For the ḥesed (faithfulness) of Yahweh is unending!

Living as we do in an increasingly cosmopolitan world, we may think that this Israelite zeal to know and honor God's name sometimes seems harsh, if not anachronistic. There is considerable appeal for many in the mystical religions of the East which declare that the divine is Unnameable. The name of God, it is said, is a limitation which reduces God to the human realm of experience, to cultural relativity; therefore all divine names (Allah, Yahweh, Brahma, Christ, etc.) point beyond to a higher order of divine Reality—to "God beyond the gods" of this world. How, then, are we to understand the announcement, found at the heart of the Torah, that the Holy God—the One who transcends our human world and is therefore beyond our naming—chooses to be known and worshiped as the One who has a personal name?

This momentous announcement is reported in the third chapter of Exodus in the story of the burning bush. Moses attempts to sidestep his commission to be God's spokesman by protesting that if he goes back to his kinsfolk in Egypt and reports a visitation from God, they will want to know, "What is his name?" (Ex. 3:13). At first the answer is given in somewhat enigmatic terms: "I WILL BE WHO I WILL BE"—a phrase which in Hebrew is a wordplay on the name "Yahweh."[5] Apparently the Israelite narrator wants to suggest that God's name is not given lightly, lest people take it in vain by attempting to manipulate and control God for their own purposes, that is, to domesticate God in their world (see the story of the golden calf, Ex. 32). But, taking this risk, so the story goes, God tells Moses to say to the Israelites that he has been sent by Yahweh, the God of the ancestors: "This is my name for ever, and thus I am to be remembered throughout all generations" (Ex. 3:15). In this manner God graciously enters into a personal "I-thou" relationship and becomes a participant in the story of the people.

The name of God, then, signifies the Holy God who turns personally to the people, whose self (or identity) is disclosed in the people's historical experience. It is significant, then, that an ancient formula for the act of worship is "to call upon the name of Yahweh." We have encountered this idiom in our previous study of psalms of lament and thanksgiving (e.g., Ps. 116:13). Indeed, the faith of the psalmists cannot be understood apart from the belief that the identity (the "who-ness") of God has been disclosed in the shared history of Israel and that the people may address God personally, by name. One psalmist says,

Those who know thy name put their trust in thee.
—Psalm 9:10 (RSV)

And to take one more illustration, in a psalm found in the Elohistic Psalter (Ps. 42-83), we should probably read in place of the general name for deity (Elohim: God):

Yahweh is known in Judah,
in Israel his name is great.
—Psalm 76:1

Two passages in the Torah (Pentateuch) may help us to understand the invocation of God by personal name. One passage is found in the context of the narrative dealing with the "root experience" of the exodus from Egypt.

> Then God [Elohim] spoke to Moses, saying to him:
> "I am Yahweh:
>   I appeared to Abraham, to Isaac, and to Jacob
>   as El Shaddai [God Almighty];
>   but by my name Yahweh I did not make myself
>   known to them."
>
> —Exodus 6:2-3

Here the narrative does not indicate that the God of the ancestors was a different god; on the contrary, the God who speaks to Moses is the same God, though now known personally by the name Yahweh. The identity of God is disclosed in the saving experience of the exodus.

The other passage, however, carries the worship of the God known by the personal name Yahweh back into the period before the ancestors Abraham, Isaac, and Jacob—indeed, to the very beginning of the primeval history. The narrator says that Adam had a son named Seth and then a grandson named Enosh.

> At that time people began to call upon the name of Yahweh.
> —Genesis 4:26b

At first glance these two traditions seem to contradict each other; but both must be taken with theological seriousness if we are to understand the usage of the personal name Yahweh in the Psalms. On the one hand, Yahweh is the God known personally in the shared history of Israel which reaches back to the crucial event of the exodus, as affirmed in the Exodus passage (Ex. 6:2-3; cf. Ex. 3:13-15). Yahweh is known in Israel as the God who liberates:

I am Yahweh your God
from the land of Egypt.
You know no God besides me,
and there is no liberator except me.
                                    —Hosea 13:4

Yet the liberating God whom Israel "knows" and worships is actually the sole and universal God, the ruler of human history and the creator of heaven and earth as affirmed in the narratives dealing with primeval history.

THE HEAVENS ARE TELLING THE GLORY OF GOD

One of the creation psalms, Psalm 19, testifies that the God whose name (identity) is known in Israel is the God whose sovereignty is evident in the cosmos.

This psalm is composed of two distinct pieces: the first (vs. 1-6) is an old hymn which praises God, the creator, whose "glory" (radiance, splendor) is displayed in the heavens. The second part (vs. 7-14) is a meditation on the Torah (Law) in which the will of Yahweh, the God known in Israel's history, is revealed. Let us consider how these two parts belong together.

In the first part of the psalm (designated Psalm 19A), the special name of God, Yahweh, is not employed. Rather, Psalm 19A seems to be an old song which praises El (translated "God" in v. 1), the ancient Semitic title for the Father of the Gods. The psalmist affirms that the phenomena of the heavens, especially the sun, are constantly proclaiming the glory of El in a great anthem of praise, inaudible to human ears.

The heavens are telling the glory of God [El];
and the firmament proclaims his handiwork.
Day to day pours forth speech,
and night to night declares knowledge.
                                    —Psalm 19:1-2 (RSV)

Night and day—like antiphonal choirs—take up the cease-less strains of the anthem of praise. Yet while this anthem is sung in the universal language of nature, it is a *silent* testi-mony which is not clearly understandable to any human being. This seems to be emphasized in the next lines:

There is no speech, nor are there words;
  their voice is not heard;
yet their voice goes out through all the earth,
  and their words to the end of the world.
                    —Psalm 19:3-4b (RSV)

The psalmist then draws upon the pagan myth of the sun-god, who at night has his abode in the mythical "sea," where he rests in the arms of his beloved, and at dawn emerges from his bridal chamber with youthful vigor and radiant splendor.

In them [i.e., the heavens] he has set a tent for the sun, which
  comes forth like a bridegroom leaving his chamber, and
  like a strong man runs its course with joy.
Its rising is from the end of the heavens,
  and its circuit to the end of them;
  and there is nothing hid from its heat.
                    —Psalm 19:4c-6 (RSV)

In these verses a deep human response to the wonder of being and of the majestic order of the cosmos, as expressed in the mythopoeic language of the ancient world, is reinterpreted to express faith in the God who is not a power of "nature" (the deified Sun) but is the creator who transcends the cosmos. The light that suffuses the universe is more than the radiance of the sun; it is the "glory" of deity—the shining light that hides God's being (cf. Isa. 6:1-3; Ezek. 1-3).

It is questionable whether the psalmist means to say

that the heavens reveal God. The celestial phenomena display God's *glory* and praise the Creator by functioning in the ordered whole, but they do not disclose who God is or God's purpose. There is a kind of knowledge of God available to human beings through contemplating the works of creation: knowledge of God's "eternal power and deity," as Paul observes in Romans 1:19-20; but it is not the saving knowledge of God's will and relationship which answers the psalmist's question: "What are human beings that you remember them?" (Ps. 8:4).

The second part of the psalm (Ps. 19B), as we have noted, is an independent literary piece. Probably it was composed much later than the first part. Yet the editorial combination of the psalms was hardly accidental. An Old Testament theologian, Gerhard von Rad, maintains that the second part was meant to be a supplement to and correction of the old hymn that draws upon mythical ideas found in the religions of the ancient world. Psalm 19B, he says, expresses "a certain doubt" that we can know God on the basis of the works of the creation. The combination of the two songs—one on the creation and the other on the *torah* (law)—is a theological testimony that "Israel's praise is directed to Yahweh's historical self-revelation given peculiarly to herself."[6] In other words, the psalm in its combined form is not concerned merely with El (deity); rather, it is based on the conviction that God has broken through the silences of nature, disclosing the divine self (name) and speaking and acting in the historical experiences of the people Israel.

This understanding of Psalm 19 is expressed in the lines of a well-known hymn by Isaac Watts (1674-1748):

The heavens declare thy glory, Lord;
In every star thy wisdom shines;
But when our eyes behold thy Word,
We read thy name in fairer lines.

For the person of faith, nature does bear impressive witness to the glory of God, but only because, first of all, in the history remembered and actualized by the believing community "we read thy name in fairer lines." Contrast the view expressed in the hymn by Joseph Addison (1672-1719) where the language reflects the faith of the Enlightenment:

> *What though in solemn silence all*
> *Move round the dark terrestrial ball?*
> *What though no real voice nor sound*
> *Amidst their radiant orbs be found?*
> *In reason's ear they all rejoice,*
> *And utter forth a glorious voice;*
> *Forever singing, as they shine,*
> *"The hand that made us is divine."*

[Addison's hymn, "The Spacious Firmament on High," is usually set to the music of a chorale from Franz Joseph Haydn's oratorio, *Creation*. The hymn, which at one point declares that "in reason's ear" the anthem of nature is heard, reflects the rationalism of the Enlightenment. Blaise Pascal (1623-1662) spoke more authentically for the modern mind when he confessed that he was torn between evidences of the Creator in nature and evidences from nature that negated his faith. See his *Pensées*, Fragment 229, The Modern Library (Random House, 1941).]

GOD WHO CREATED A PEOPLE

Our study of the relationship between the two parts of Psalm 19 provides an avenue of approach to other psalms in which Yahweh is extolled as creator. To understand Israel's creation faith sympathetically it is best to start with psalms that praise Yahweh as the God who created a people out of the historical nothingness of slavery and gave them a future and a vocation. This view of creation as the formation of a community is deeply rooted in Israelite tradition. It is found in ancient Israelite poetry, for instance, in the Song of the Sea (Ex. 15:1-18), which has been discussed earlier (Chapter 2). In this poem the event of the deliverance at the Reed Sea is portrayed in imagery that reflects the old myth of the Creator's conflict with the powers of chaos. Addressing Yahweh, the singer speaks of

> the people whom you have redeemed (Ex. 15:13)

and

> the people whom you have created[7] (Ex. 15:16).

It is striking that here redemption and creation are blended together. Creation is not understood as a cosmic event—the creation of heaven and earth—but as a historical event of liberation.

This view of creation is expressed in the various hymns listed above under the caption "Hymns to God, Who Created (Redeemed) Israel," such as Psalm 114 ("When Israel went forth from Egypt"), or the familiar psalm often called "Old Hundredth."

Know that it is Yahweh who is God!
  He made us and to him we belong;
We are his people,
  the flock of his pasture.
                    —Psalm 100:2

The affirmation "Yahweh is our creator" has its counterpart in the confession that "we are his" (probably the correct reading of the Hebrew at this point) and therefore dependent, like a flock, upon the shepherd.

A beautiful example of this view of creation is found in Psalm 74, a lament in which a hymnic passage (vs. 12-17) is included as an expression of confidence in time of distress. Since the psalm is found in the Elohistic Psalter

(Ps. 42-83), we may assume that originally the hymn was addressed not to "God" in general but to the God known personally by the name Yahweh.

Yet God [Yahweh] my King is from of old,
working salvation in the midst of the earth.
Thou didst divide the sea by thy might;
thou didst break the heads of the dragons on the waters.
Thou didst crush the heads of Leviathan,
thou didst give him as food for the creatures of the
wilderness.

—Psalm 74:12-14 (RSV)

In the ensuing lines the poet moves to the subject of creation in a cosmic sense: the creation of day and night, the heavenly bodies, brooks and springs, summer and winter. Notice, however, that initially the poet effectively employs the old creation myth of the Divine Warrior's victory over the multiheaded dragon, Leviathan (cf. Isa. 27:1), to portray the crucial event at the Reed Sea when a people was redeemed from powers of chaos. Yahweh's saving deed at the sea was also an act of creation.

Outside the Psalter the prophet known as Second Isaiah (Isa. 40-55) resorts to hymnic poetry to proclaim that Yahweh, the God whom Israel worships, is both Creator and Redeemer. This poet also understands creation, in one sense, as the creation of a people, for Yahweh is identified as

the One who created you, O Jacob,
who formed you, O Israel.
—Isaiah 43:1; also v. 7

Accordingly, in a lyrical poem in which the poet gives an apostrophe to the powerful "arm of Yahweh," the event of the exodus at the Reed Sea is portrayed in mythopoeic language as the time when the Divine Warrior created (redeemed) a people. And this event in poetic imagination typifies the new exodus of salvation that is about to occur.

> Awake, awake! Clothe yourself in strength,
>   arm of Yahweh!
> Awake, as in the past,
>   in times of generations long ago.
> Did you not split Rahab in two,
>   and pierce the Dragon through?
> Did you not dry up the Sea,
>   the waters of the great Abyss,
> to make the seabed a road,
>   for the redeemed to cross?
>   —Isaiah 51:9-10 (JB)

In the prophet's view, Yahweh is the Creator/Redeemer of Israel who creates "the new thing" in history (Isa. 43:19) because, in a larger sense, Yahweh is the Creator of the cosmos (Isa. 40:2-23, 25-26; 45:9-13). The Creator whom Israel worships transcends the whole sweep of time and, being "the first" and "the last" (Isa. 48:12), can grasp the drama of history in its totality, from beginning to end.

THE MAJESTIC NAME

In the foregoing discussion we have seen that Israel's praise is not directed to "deity" in a general sense but to the God whose identity or "name" is known in the shared history of the people. This discussion has prepared us to consider a number of hymns in which the people praise Yahweh as the Creator of the cosmos and the Ruler of history.

The exquisite Psalm 8 is a hymn of praise to the Creator. Notice the hymnic pattern:

A. Invocation
    The psalm begins with an exclamation of praise to "Yahweh, our Ruler" (Lord), whose name is great

throughout the whole earth. The initial address to Yahweh is expanded by a "who" clause (vs. 1b-2) which portrays the divine majesty in the heavens. The details are not clear, but apparently the poet depicts Yahweh's splendid "bulwark" or celestial palace (temple) above the firmament, from which Yahweh comes to subdue foes that threaten the divine rule.

B. Motive for Praise

The motive for praise is introduced in v. 3 with the transitional particle *ki*, here translated "when." The poet reflects on what it means to "know" Yahweh personally, by name. Looking up at the star-studded night sky, the psalmist is overwhelmed with a sense of the relatively ephemeral and weak character of human beings and wonders why the Creator pays any attention to such infinitesimally tiny creatures.

When I survey your heavens, your fingerworks,
the moon and the stars that you have established,
what are human beings that you consider them,
human persons that you seek them out?

The psalmist's question does not stand by itself but is followed by a contrasting statement, introduced by an adversative "yet." Such an insignificant creature, yet one whom Yahweh has elevated to a high role in the Creator's cosmic administration! The language has affinities with the climax of the Genesis creation story (Gen. 1:26-27).

Yet you have placed them slightly below heavenly beings,
and with honor and majesty have crowned them.

You have given them dominion over your handiwork,
 everything you have put in subjection to them:
 sheep and oxen altogether, wild beasts also,
 birds of the air and fish of the sea,
 everything that courses through the waterways.
                                                —Psalm 8:3-6

  C. Refrain
      In the typical style of the hymn, the poem is
      rounded off by sounding the note struck at the
      beginning:

O Yahweh, our Sovereign,
 how majestic is your name throughout the earth!

    Psalm 8 deals with two inseparably related questions:
the question of who God is, and the question of the role of
human beings in God's creation. The psalm is closely
related to the creation story in Genesis 1, a fact that is not
surprising when one considers that both have their setting
in the worship of the Jerusalem Temple. The psalmist's
affirmation that Yahweh has created human beings so that
they fall short "just a little" from the divine status of
Elohim ("God" or, more likely in this case, "heavenly
beings") is parallel to the statement made in the Genesis
creation story that God made human beings "in the image
of God" (Gen. 1:26-27). In both cases the intention of the
writer is to say that human beings are made for *relationship*
with God, a relationship that elevates them above the
natural world and enables them to have dominion over
"nature." Contrast the psalmist's question of amazement
about the human role in God's creation with the same
question in Psalm 144:3-4 (cf. Job 7:17-18), where the
emphasis is on human transience.

    [The word Elohim in Ps. 8:5 may refer to "the sons of God"
    or heavenly beings who, according to the ancient pictorial

way of thinking, surround God in the heavenly court. This view may be presupposed in Gen. 1:26, where the plural forms ("Let us . . . in our image") suggest that God is addressing the heavenly council (cf. I Kings 22:19). The Greek translation of the Old Testament (Septuagint) reads "angels" at Ps. 8:5, and this interpretation is adopted in the Epistle to the Hebrews (2:6-8) where the psalm is quoted.]

This view of human dominion over nature is revolutionary when measured against ancient religions which portrayed the gods as forces within the cosmos and which regarded human life as embraced within the order of creation, with its rhythmic cycles of the seasons and its mysterious power of life (fertility) and death. The God whom Israel worships, Yahweh, is not a power within the cosmos. Rather, as Creator, Yahweh transcends the cosmos and hence is "Ruler of all nature," to use an expression from the Crusader's Hymn, "Fairest Lord Jesus." And in a lesser sense human beings, though related to their natural environment (as shown by the creation stories at the beginning of the Bible), stand over against nature as creatures who are given the high calling to have dominion over the works of God's creation. They are to "image" or represent the rule (kingdom) of God on earth.

Let us pause to reflect on the implications of this biblical theology of creation. The biblical view, which emptied "nature" of divinity, opened the way for a "scientific" approach to nature as a realm that human beings can study and explore and whose resources can be used in God-given stewardship ("to till and keep" the garden, Gen. 2:15). It is hardly accidental that the scientific movement, which has brought about revolutionary developments in the twentieth century on earth and in space, has been nourished in the soil of the biblical tradition. The tremendous achievements of science in the fields of medicine, transportation, communication, and space exploration—to mention only a few—may be regarded as a partial fulfillment of the task that the Creator has given human beings in crowning them to have dominion over the earthly realm of creation.

The other side of this picture, of course, is the biblical portrayal of the risk that God has taken in elevating human beings to a high role of responsibility in the creation. This risk is portrayed in the story of Paradise Lost (Gen. 2-3), which is included as a supplement to the creation story in the final canonical edition of the Torah (Pentateuch). The biblical narrative shows that the position of dominion over the natural world may tempt human beings to assert their independence vis-à-vis God, and to use their God-given freedom in such a manner that the earth becomes a scene of exploitation, warfare, and chaos. The biblical narrators give us no simple assurance that human beings, who fall just short of divine status, will use their honored position to execute God's purpose on the earth and to order social life in accordance with God's will. This is the fundamental problem to which the opening chapters of the Bible are addressed: human grandeur and human misery, the high calling and the lost opportunity.

In our own time we can sense this human problem clearly as we see how science, which could be the form of imaging God's rule on earth, holds the terrifying possibility of nuclear destruction of the earth and of carrying military adventures into space. Moreover, we have been made painfully aware of the fact that human exploitation of the earth's resources may upset the balance of nature, with the result that the earth will no longer be a habitable place for human and animal life. The question is whether human beings—as scientists, industrialists, or technologists—can fulfill the high calling that was given to humanity by the Creator.

An exquisite expression of Israel's creation faith is found in Psalm 104, a hymn that has many affinities with the Genesis creation story. As in Psalm 8, which we have just considered, the poet's praise is directed to Yahweh ("O Yahweh, my God"), whose name is great in the earth. In composing this poem, the poet has drawn upon mythopoeic motifs known outside Israel. Indeed, at points this psalm displays striking resemblance in style and content to "The Hymn to the Aton," composed by the Pharaoh Akhenaton, the reforming Egyptian king of the fourteenth century B.C. who introduced a kind of monotheism based on the worship of the benevolent divine power symbolized by the sun disc. (See the discussion of this Egyptian hymn in Chapter 2.) Moreover, the poet has made use of the myth of the Creator's subduing the powers of chaos which was known in Mesopotamia and particularly in the Canaanite (Ugaritic) literature from the fourteenth century B.C.[8]

A. Invocation
   In the style of a hymn, Psalm 104 begins (v. 1a) with an invocation addressed to the poet's *nefesh*, that is, self or being. All the powers of one's being in their psychosomatic unity are invited to join in praising Yahweh. In this respect it is like Psalm 103, a hymn (see above, pp. 127-130), which opens on the same note.

B. Motive for Praise
   The invocation to praise Yahweh leads into the main body of the psalm (vs. 2-30) which provides the motive for praise. The elaboration of the ground for praise is developed in seven strophes which follow the sequence of the Genesis creation story (see chart, p. 158). The poet ascribes praise in

a series of "who" clauses: Yahweh is the One who stretched out the heavens, who set the earth on its foundations, etc. Notice how the poet employs, much more freely than in the Genesis creation story, the ancient myth about the conflict between the Creator and the powers of chaos, symbolized by the raging sea, insurgent waters or floods, or the monster sometimes called Rahab or Leviathan (see Ps. 89:10; 74:13-14; Job 9:18; 26:12). The earth, we are told, is firmly established in the midst of the primeval waters, but the waters appear to be unruly, hostile, threatening. The waters symbolize the powers of chaos which the Creator has to "rebuke," "chase back," limit and hold within bounds. In the poetic ascription, Yahweh is the One—

Who establishes Earth upon her foundations,
  so that she is immovable for ever.
With *Tehom* **[watery abyss] you covered her like a garment,**
  above the mountains the waters stood.
From your rebuke they fled,
  from your thundering voice they fled away.
The mountains rose, the valleys sank down
  to the place which you determined for them.
A limit you fixed which they are not to transgress,
  never again to cover the earth.
                          —Psalm 104:5-9

Later on, we hear that "the sea, great and vast" is not threatening, for it teems with marine life, ships ply their course through it, and the mythical monster of chaos (Leviathan; think of *Moby Dick!*) is only a zoological creature that Yahweh has formed to sport around in the water (vs. 25-26).

THE "ORDER" OF CREATION

Strophe i
Ps. 104:2-4
Gen. 1:6-8

In pictorial language the poet speaks of God's "stretching out" the heavens and laying the foundations of the heavenly palace on the cosmic ocean above the firmament.

Strophe ii
Ps. 104:5-9
Gen. 1:9-10

God has firmly established the earth by putting the rebellious waters of chaos to flight and establishing bounds for them so that chaos would not engulf the earth.

Strophe iii
Ps. 104:10-13
Implied in
Gen. 1:6-10

The chaotic waters, having been tamed, were converted to beneficial use. The waters gush up from underground springs and pour down in rain from the sky.

Strophe iv
Ps. 104:14-18
Gen. 1:11-12

As a result, vegetation flourishes, which makes life possible for birds, beasts, and human beings.

Strophe v
Ps. 104:19-23
Gen. 1:14-18

God created the moon and the sun to mark the rhythm of seasons and of day and night, so that beasts may seek food during the darkness and human beings may perform their work in daylight.

Strophe vi
Ps. 104:24-26
Gen. 1:20-22

The poet reflects upon the remnant of watery chaos: the sea, which teems with creatures great and small. Leviathan is no longer the dreaded monster of chaos, but is God's "plaything" (cf. Job 41:5).

Strophe vii
Ps. 104:27-30
Gen. 1:24-30

The dependence of human beings and animals upon God, their Creator, for life.

Here we are given a picture of the marvelous order and design of God's creation: a carefully wrought whole in which all creatures, including human beings, have their proper place and time. The poet contemplates the rich diversity of creation and marvels at the divine wisdom (v. 24) evident in the wonderful whole. There is even an element of aesthetic enjoyment in this poem—a feeling for the beauty of God's creation. This experience of beauty, however, is not based merely on human perception. The psalm is a commentary on God's approving judgment that the creation as a whole and in all its parts is "very good" (Gen. 1:31). This is God's world, marred only by human wickedness, a melancholy note struck in the concluding refrain of the poem (vs. 31-35; see especially v. 35). Human enjoyment may be full because God "rejoices" in the works of creation.

C. Concluding Refrain

In good hymnic style the psalm concludes by striking the note of invocation sounded at the beginning, thus rounding off the whole (v. 35c).

[The concluding "Hallelu-jah" ("Praise Yah[weh]" actually belongs with the following psalm. This transposition means that both Psalm 105 and 106 are hallelujah psalms (see Ps. 111-118), each beginning and usually ending with the liturgical exclamation.]

The high point of Psalm 104 is reached in a passage (vs. 27-30) that comes just before the concluding refrain. Psalm 8, it will be recalled, followed the Genesis creation story by stressing the supremacy of human beings in God's earthly creation. This note is lacking in Psalm 104. Instead, the poet stresses the equality of human beings and animals, who together depend upon the Creator. It is difficult to catch the full meaning of this passage in English translation. In the original Hebrew, the verbs indicate action that is incomplete, continuing, frequentive. This meaning can be rendered into English only by using the present tense, which is often used for actions that are repeated.

All of them [animals and humans] look to you
to give them their food in its season.
When you give to them, they gather up;
when you open your hand, they are satisfied to the full.
When you hide your face, they are disturbed,
when you take away their breath, they expire
and return to their dust.
When you send forth your spirit, they are [re]created,
and you renew the surface of the soil.
—Psalm 104:27-30

In this psalm the emphasis falls upon *creatio continua*. Creation is not just an event that occurred in the beginning but is God's continuing activity of sustaining creatures and holding everything in being. The cosmos is not a self-existent whole, perpetuated through its own internally operating dynamic. On the contrary, the whole order of being is radically dependent on God, the Creator. If for an instant God were to "hide his face" or to "withdraw his *ruah*" ("breath," "wind," "spirit"), to use the psalmist's poetic language, then every being would languish and fall back into primeval chaos.

Of course, this is the language of religious poetry, not that of science. Yet this poetic language expresses in a profound way the universal human experience that existence is contingent—suspended, as it were, over the abyss. Modern poets, novelists, and philosophers have also portrayed the depth dimension of existence and

The desperate catabasis
Into the snarl of the abyss
That always lies just underneath

Our jolly picnic on the heath
Of the agreeable . . .
                        —W. H. Auden[9]

Another psalmist begins by announcing that the earth
and all it contains is radically contingent, for Yahweh has
founded it upon the waters of chaos.

To Yahweh belongs the earth and everything in it,
the world and those who inhabit it.

Then comes the motive for hymnic praise, stated in
mythopoeic imagery:

For [ki] he has founded it upon seas,
and established it upon floods.
                        —Psalm 24:1

The remainder of this psalm contains a liturgy that reflects
worship at the Temple of Jerusalem (to be considered in
the next chapter).

PRAISE TO YAHWEH FROM THE ENDS OF THE EARTH

The use of mythopoeic imagery which expresses the
depth dimension of human existence shows that there is a
universalism in Israel's worship of Yahweh. The psalmists' praise of Yahweh does not lead to a theological
confinement with Israel's history but, rather, to a spacious
view that embraces all peoples and the whole cosmos. For
the God whose name (identity) was disclosed in Israel's
historical experience is the God upon whom all human
beings, and all forms of creaturely existence, are
dependent. The word that was spoken to Israel is the truth
that illumines the meaning of all human life. Thus the
hymnic invocation to praise Yahweh is addressed, not just
to Israel, but to all peoples and to "the ends of the earth."

Sing a new hymn to Yahweh!
Let his praise resound from the ends of the earth,
let the sea and all that it holds sing his praises,
the islands and those who inhabit them.

Let the desert and its cities raise their voice,
the camp where Kedar lives.
Let the inhabitants of Sela cry aloud
and shout from the mountain tops.
Let them give glory to Yahweh
and let the people of the islands voice his praise.
              —*Isaiah 42:10-12 (JB)*

Even the most remote and isolated places—Kedar (Jer. 49:28-29) and Sela (II Kings 14:7)—are embraced within the meaning of history which Yahweh discloses.

It is therefore significant that some of Israel's hymns move without a break from the praise of Yahweh the Creator to the praise of Yahweh as the Lord of history. We have already found this to be the case in a storytelling psalm like Psalm 136, which departs from the outline of Israel's credo by prefixing to the sacred history the rehearsal of Yahweh's great deeds of creation (Ps. 136:4-9). This kind of praise finds even more magnificent expression in Psalm 33, whose central theme is that Yahweh is enthroned as celestial King (Ps. 33:14) and therefore is Creator and Lord of the earth.

This psalm also displays the characteristic form of a hymn.

  A. Invocation
      The psalm begins (vs. 1-3) by summoning the community to praise Yahweh and to sing "a new song" to the accompaniment of musical instruments.

  B. Motive for Praise
      The main section (vs. 4-19), introduced by "for" (*ki*), announces the motive for praise.

For the word of Yahweh is just,
and all his work is done faithfully.
He loves righteousness and justice,
the faithfulness [ḥesed] of Yahweh fills the
earth.

—Psalm 33:4-5

The psalmist expands this theme by saying, first, that it was by the "word of Yahweh" that the heavens and the earth were made (vs. 6-9); and second, by declaring that "the counsel of Yahweh" is the determining power in human history (vs. 10-18). The psalmist refers to the special relationship between Yahweh and Israel, "the people whom he has chosen as his heritage" (v. 12), but concentrates on Yahweh's sovereignty over all nations (vs. 13-15). In this poet's view, to be a nation "under God" means abandoning trust in military arms (vs. 16-17).

C. Concluding Refrain
The psalm concludes with an expression of trust in Yahweh, Creator and Redeemer (vs. 20-22), thereby resounding the note struck at the beginning.

The spacious universalism of this psalm does not contradict the conviction that God's name (self, identity) has been disclosed in the community of Israel. On the contrary, Yahweh's historical self-disclosure to Israel provides the basis for the universal horizons of thought. The revelation (word) of Yahweh is not only the inner meaning of the events of Israel's history; it is also the meaning of every individual's experience (see especially Ps. 103 and 113), the meaning of human history, and the meaning of the whole cosmos.

By the word of Yahweh the heavens were made,
  their whole array by the breath of his mouth;
he collects the ocean waters as though in a wineskin,
  he stores the deeps in cellars.

Let the whole world fear Yahweh,
  let all who live on earth revere him!
He spoke, and it was created;
  he commanded, and there it stood.

—Psalm 33:6-9 (JB)

Creation by the word is expressed also in the hymn Psalm 148 (see vs. 5-6) and, of course, in the liturgical prose of the Genesis creation story. From this point it is not a far cry to the announcement made at the opening of the Gospel of John. Echoing the "in the beginning" of Genesis 1:1, this Gospel affirms that God's revelation in Christ was the Word by whom all things were created and in whom all things are sustained. And this Word is not confined to a corner of history: it is "the true light that enlightens every human being" (John 1:9).

NOTES

1. Otto Eissfeldt, *The Old Testament: An Introduction* (Harper & Row, 1965), pp. 105-106.
2. Helmer Ringgren, in his study *The Faith of the Psalmists* (Fortress Press, 1963), emphasizes this aspect of visual participation in the ritual drama: "The creation and the exodus from Egypt were not only great and precious memories treasured by the faithful and now and then recollected or commemorated. They were events that were actualized and re-experienced whenever the great festivals were celebrated in the temple" (p. 90). See also the ensuing discussion.
3. Some of these ancient hymns are found in James B. Pritchard (ed.), *Ancient Near Eastern Texts Relating to the Old Testament*, 3d ed. (Princeton University Press, 1969), pp. 365-401.
4. See the discussion of "Name" in Johannes Pedersen, *Israel: Its*

Life and Culture, Vols. 1-2 (London: Oxford University Press, 1926, 1959), pp. 245-259.

5. Translated in the Revised Standard Version as "I AM WHO I AM" (Ex. 3:14). An illuminating discussion of the name of God is given by Gerhard von Rad in his little book *Moses,* World Christian Books (Association Press, 1960), Ch. 2.

6. See Gerhard von Rad, *Old Testament Theology,* Vol. 1, trans. D. M. G. Stalker (Harper & Row, 1962), p. 362.

7. Translating the verb *qana* as "create" rather than "purchase." See Frank M. Cross, "The Song of the Sea and Canaanite Myth," in *Canaanite Myth and Hebrew Epic* (Harvard University Press, 1973).

8. On the reinterpretation of mythical symbolism in hymns of creation, see further Bernhard W. Anderson, *Creation Versus Chaos* (Association Press, 1967), Ch. 3, "Creation and Worship." A basic work on the mythical view of reality is Mircea Eliade, *Cosmos and History: The Myth of the Eternal Return,* trans. Willard R. Trask (Harper & Brothers, 1959).

9. W. H. Auden, *New Year Letter* (London: Faber & Faber, 1941), p. 40. In the' Epilogue to my *Creation Versus Chaos* (pp. 171-177) I give further examples of the modern use of the symbolism of the chaos myth.

6
BE STILL
AND KNOW

With few exceptions the psalms considered in the previous chapters—the laments, thanksgivings, and hymns—may be called "cultic songs." These songs were designed for, or at least presupposed, a setting of worship in which the cultic community responded to the overtures of God toward the people in their ongoing history.[1] Of course, not *all* the psalms were intended for use on cultic occasions in the Temple. Some were intended for the circles of home or palace, some were to be sung by pilgrims on their journey or by workers in the field, some were for teaching or private meditation and reflection. In many ways, however, the psalms express the longing of the Israelite to "behold the face of God," that is, to be present at the Temple, where Yahweh is "enthroned on the praises of Israel" (Ps. 22:3). This yearning is expressed passionately in one of the laments:

**As a deer longs for streams of water,
  so my whole being longs for you, Yahweh.***
**My being thirsts for God,
  for the living God.**
**When shall I go to see
  the face of God?**

  —Psalm 42:1-2

---

*This psalm stands at the beginning of the Elohistic Psalter (Ps. 42-83); we would expect to read the personal name Yahweh here (as in an ancient version).

The psalmist's consuming desire is to "dwell" (sojourn, visit) in the house of Yahweh (cf. Ps. 23:6), that is, to worship in the Temple.

> One thing I ask of Yahweh,
>   that I seek:
> To dwell in the house of Yahweh
>   all the days of my life,
> to contemplate the favor of Yahweh,
>   and to inquire in his temple.
>   —Psalm 27:4

The verbs of seeing used in these poetic contexts ("behold the face," "contemplate," or "gaze on") are intriguing. Outside of Israel language like this would refer to something very concrete: beholding the god's statue in the temple or in a ceremonial procession. However, since Israelite religion from the time of Moses prohibited statues (Ex. 20:4), this visual interpretation is excluded. Some have suggested that expressions like "seeing God's power and glory" (Ps. 63:2) may refer to a cultic drama or "liturgical mime" in which God's deeds were enacted.[2] Or, of course, the visual language, at least in many cases, is merely a metaphorical expression for the nearness of God experienced in the Temple services. In any case, the Temple is the particular place where God's glory "dwells" (Ps. 26:8). Therefore a psalmist prays:

> Send forth your light and your truth,
>   let them guide me,
> let them escort me to your holy hill,
>   to your tabernacle.
> Then I will come to the altar of God,
>   to God my delightful joy,
> and praise you on the harp,
>   O Yahweh my God.   —Psalm 43:3-4

[The last line translated reads redundantly in the Hebrew, "O God, my God." This psalm, however, is the opening psalm in the so-called Elohistic Psalter which prefers to substitute the general term "God" for the personal name Yahweh. Following the Greek translation (Septuagint), we should read here "Yahweh, my God."]

The psalms, then, lend no support to the notion that a person's relationship with God is a private affair and that God is accessible outside the liturgical forms and sacraments of the worshiping community. On the contrary, the individual is related to God as a member of the covenant community. To be sure, God is not bound by the limitations of the community but can deal with people freely and graciously (see Ex. 33:19). Yet if persons would have access to God in worship—if they would "call upon the name of Yahweh," to recall the idiom discussed in the last chapter, then they must come to the established meeting place with others and engage in a corporate form of worship. In the Psalter, therefore, the individual praises God in concert with the worshiping community.

O praise Yahweh with me,
and let us exalt his name together!
—Psalm 34:3

LITURGIES OF THE TRIBAL FEDERATION

In the period before the formation of the state under David, when Israel was loosely bound together as a tribal confederacy, it was customary for people to gather from all the tribes of Israel to the central sanctuary, located first at Shechem (Josh. 24) and subsequently at Shiloh (I Sam. 1). The ancient covenant law specifically enjoined three annual pilgrimages, at which times the representatives of the people "must appear before the Suzerain ['Adon] Yahweh" (Ex. 23:14-17; 34:18, 22-23). These pilgrimage festivals, originally adopted from the Canaanite sacred calendar, coincided with the major agricultural seasons. The first, the Festival of Unleavened Bread (later associated with the Passover), was held in March-April at the time of the barley harvest; the second, the Festival of First Fruits (also called Weeks or Pentecost), occurred in May-June at the time of the wheat harvest; and the third, the Festival of Ingathering (also called Tabernacles), took place in September-October at the time of the grape and olive harvest.

Of these three festivals, the most important was the autumn vintage festival. This wine festival, held at the turn of the year according to the old agricultural calendar (and later connected with New Year's Day: Rosh ha-Shana), was celebrated with dancing and merrymaking (Judg. 21:19-23). It was a time of drinking new wine, to judge from Eli's suspicion that Hannah was "drunken" (I Sam. 1:14-15). However, what had originated as a Canaanite nature festival was radically transformed by being reinterpreted in terms of Israel's historical experiences. The custom—which has continued to the present day—of making huts or booths out of tree branches and erecting them in the vineyards while the grapes were being harvested, was reinterpreted as a commemoration of the time in the wilderness when Israel lived in huts or shelters (Lev. 23:43). (The Latin Vulgate translated the Hebrew word *sukkoth*, "huts" or "booths," as *tabernacula*, from which comes our word "tabernacles.")

Even in a very early period, before the time of David, the Israelites seem to have celebrated this festival as a time for renewing the covenant with Yahweh. In the service of worship the saving deeds of Yahweh in Israel's history were proclaimed, and the people were called upon to reaffirm their allegiance to the God of Israel. The structure of this covenant renewal service has been reconstructed from Joshua 24 and related passages as follows:[3]

1. The call to assembly (Josh. 24:1)
2. Historical prologue: a confessional summary of Yahweh's deeds of deliverance (Josh. 24:2-13)
3. Call to decision for or against Yahweh (Josh. 24:14-22)
4. Purification: removal of foreign gods (Josh. 24:23-24; cf. Gen. 35:1-4)
5. The renewal of the covenant (Josh. 24:25; cf. Ex. 24:4-8)
6. The reading of the covenant law (Josh. 24:25-26; cf. Ex. 24:7)
7. A ceremony of sanctions: the blessings and the curses (see Deut. 27:11-26; Josh. 8:30-35)
8. The dismissal of the congregation (Josh. 24:28)

Some of the elements of this covenant renewal service are present in contemporary worship services. It would be interesting to compare the form of this service with the Covenant Renewal Service of John Wesley, designed primarily for use at the turn of the year.[4]

This liturgical tradition persisted even after the unity of the Davidic kingdom was broken and the people were politically divided into North Israel (Ephraim) and South Israel (Judah). According to I Kings 12:32-33, Jeroboam I (931-910 B.C.), the first king of North Israel, instituted an autumn festival "like the feast that was in Judah"—a reference to the harvest or New Year festival (Tabernacles) which was celebrated in the south. For political reasons he wanted to deter his people from making pilgrimages to the Temple in Jerusalem, and so he revived the old covenant renewal festival that had been celebrated during the days of the tribal confederacy (the time of the Judges). Subsequently, Bethel became one of the major cultic centers in the north, a fact recognized by the prophet Amos more than a century later when he traveled from his home in the south to Bethel, where "a temple of the kingdom" was located (Amos 7:13). Amos' contemporary, Hosea, seems to have referred to the fall festival in the north (Hos. 9:5, "the day of the feast of Yahweh"). Undoubtedly some of the psalms now found in the Psalter were used in the Bethel cult. A good example of a North Israelite psalm is the community lament found in Psalm 80 which begins with an address to Yahweh, "Shepherd of Israel," and then, shifting metaphors, speaks of the people as Yahweh's vineyard:

Thou didst bring a vine out of Egypt;
   thou didst drive out the nations and plant it.
Thou didst clear the ground for it;
   it took deep root and filled the land.
The mountains were covered with its shade,
   the mighty cedars with its branches;
it sent out its branches to the sea,
   and its shoots to the [Euphrates] River.
                    —Psalm 80:8-11 (RSV)

It may be surmised that, after the fall of the Northern Kingdom under Assyrian aggression in 722 B.C., these psalms were taken over in South Israel (Judah), where they were adapted for use in the festivals of Zion.

It is difficult to tell which psalms actually belonged to the covenant renewal festival. In his commentary on the Psalms, Artur Weiser assigns a great number to this festival, but he surely goes too far.[5] Many of the psalms so classified belong to the Zion festival (to be considered presently), which emphasized God's covenant with David and the choice of Zion. Two psalms, however, seem to reflect liturgies of covenant renewal.

COVENANT RENEWAL LITURGIES

50 "I will accept no bull from your house"
*81 "Hear, O my people, while I admonish you!"

Captions are from the RSV.

Notice that Psalm 81 closely parallels the liturgy of covenant renewal found in Joshua 24. It begins with an invocation to praise "the God of Jacob" at the sanctuary "on our feast day," presumably a reference to the fall festival (vs. 1-5a). Then comes a reminder, perhaps given by a cultic priest or prophet, of what Yahweh has done for the people, beginning with the deliverance from Egyptian bondage (vs. 5b-10). The psalm reaches a climax with an appeal to the people to repent and reaffirm their loyalty to Yahweh, and to "walk in my [Yahweh's] ways" (vs. 11-16), that is, to accept anew the duties of the covenant law. The theological assumption of Psalm 81 is that of the Mosaic covenant: "*If* you will obey my voice and keep my covenant, you shall be my own possession among all peoples" (Ex. 19:5). This conditional covenant carries consequences which prophets like Hosea spelled out clearly: disobedience results in divine judgment and the dissolution of the covenant relationship—"You are not my people and I am not your God" (Hos. 1:8b). According to this Mosaic covenant theology, the sufferings and evils of history are traced to a fault in the human will. Those who "sow the wind" shall "reap the whirlwind" (Hos. 8:7) in the historical arena.

THE FESTIVAL OF ZION

Psalms like these may go back to a liturgical tradition of the tribal confederacy that was kept alive in North Israel (Ephraim). The Psalter in its present form, however, has been shaped in the circles of South Israel (Judah) and represents the liturgical usage of the Jerusalem Temple where Yahweh was acclaimed hymnically as King over Israel, the nations, and the cosmos.

The theme of the kingdom (kingship) of God, which was the burden of Jesus' preaching according to early gospel tradition (Mark 1:14-15), is deeply rooted in Israel's history of worship, going back to a time long before Israel had an earthly king. The ancient hymn found in Ex. 15:1-18, the Song of the Sea, concludes with the exclamation:

> Let Yahweh be King for ever and ever!
> —Ex. 15:18b

In the period of the tribal confederacy the confession that Yahweh is King was maintained tenaciously, especially in conservative circles that resisted the introduction of monarchy "like the nations" (Judg. 8:22-23; I Sam. 8:4-22). Even after the monarchy was founded under the leadership of Saul and especially David, this ancient confession persisted and received great prominence in the Jerusalem Temple services. According to the report of Isaiah's call, it was in the Temple that the prophet caught a vision of Yahweh, *the* King par excellence enthroned upon a celestial throne, whose glory fills the whole earth (Isa. 6:1-5).

The theme of Yahweh's kingship is central in a cluster of psalms that seem to reflect a great religious festival celebrated in "Zion," a term that referred originally to the fortified ridge captured by David but soon came to include the adjacent Temple area and eventually the whole city of Jerusalem. All the psalms belonging to this category are hymns. A prominent feature is the cultic exclamation *Yahweh malak,* usually translated "Yahweh reigns" or "Yahweh is King."

ENTHRONEMENT PSALMS

29 "Enthroned as king for ever"
✓*47 "God is the king of all the earth"
93 "Thy throne is established from of old"

*95 "A great King above all gods"
*96 "Declare his glory among the nations!"
97   "Thou art exalted far above all gods"
*98 "The ends of the earth have seen the victory of
      our God"
*99 "Mighty King, lover of justice"

(See also Psalm 24, an entrance liturgy.)

Captions are from the RSV.

These hymns presuppose the centrality of Zion, where
Yahweh is magnified in the praises of the people (see,
e.g., Ps. 96:6; 97:8; 99:2, 9). It is clear, however, that
Yahweh's rule is not confined to Zion. The whole earth,
indeed the entire sphere of creation, is full of the King's
glory. In these psalms the particularities of Israel's
historical experience as the people of Yahweh are
noticeably sublimated, if not ignored, except for a few pale
allusions (e.g., Ps. 99:6-8). In Zion the God of Israel is
extolled as the king of the nations and of the universe.
According to one text, it seems that the peoples of the
earth, represented by their princes, have become members of the People of God.

God reigns over the nations;
  God sits on his holy throne.
The princes of the peoples gather
  as the people of the God of Abraham.
For the shields [rulers] of the earth belong to God;
  he is highly exalted!

                              —Psalm 47:8-9 (RSV)

[Again it should be noted that at this point we are in the
Elohistic Psalter and that originally this psalm celebrated the
kingship of Yahweh, not "God" in general.]

In the festival of Zion the kingship of Yahweh was not
just announced, it was celebrated in a ritual enactment of

Yahweh's enthronement. A passage in Psalm 47, the psalm just quoted, announces that Yahweh has "gone up" (ascended the throne) amid shouts of acclamation and with the sound of the trumpet (*shofar*):

God has gone up with a shout [of acclamation],
Yahweh, to the sound of the *shofar*!
Sing praises to our God, sing praises;
sing praises to our King, sing praises.
For King of the whole earth is God,
sing hymns of praise.
God reigns over the nations,
God sits on his holy throne.

—Psalm 47:5-8

This passage seems to refer to the bearing of the Ark of the Covenant in procession to the Temple (Ps. 24:7-10) where Yahweh "sits enthroned upon the cherubim" (Ps. 99:1), the winged figures that flanked the Ark. Since, however, the earthly temple was regarded as a microcosmic copy of the heavenly one, as in Isaiah's vision, the drama symbolized Yahweh's entrance into the heavenly palace (temple) and the ascension to the celestial throne. Thus Yahweh, "the great King" (Ps. 47:2), not only reigns in Israel, where earthly praises are sung, but over the whole cosmos.

The psalms of Yahweh's enthronement may reflect a festival held in the fall, at the turn of the year, when worshipers made a pilgrimage to Jerusalem to celebrate Yahweh's kingly triumph over all powers hostile to the divine rule. This view has been championed with considerable persuasiveness by the Scandinavian scholar Sigmund Mowinckel, who—with excessive enthusiasm —assigns some twenty psalms to this category (Ps. 8; 15; 24; 29; 33; 46; 48; 50; 66A; 75; 76; 81; 82; 84; 95; 100; 114; 118; 132; 149). In his view the fall festival celebrated in

Jerusalem was patterned after festivals of divine kingship known among Israel's neighbors.[6]

The chief example is the Babylonian New Year festival, the *akitu*, at which the Babylonian creation myth was recited and reenacted. The myth depicts the violent struggle between the young god Marduk, and the goddess Tiamat, the dragon of chaos, and her chaotic allies. Victorious in the conflict, the divine warrior was acclaimed king in the council of the gods and the hymnic cry was raised: "Marduk has become king." The myth portrays human involvement in the processes of nature which, moving in a circle, ever return to the beginning when the god must win a new victory over the powers of darkness and chaos.

Since Israel's worship was profoundly influenced by the surrounding culture, it is tempting to interpret these enthronement psalms in the light of cultic practice in Mesopotamia and Canaan. Some scholars argue that the cultic exclamation *Yahweh malak* should be translated, "Yahweh has become King," in which case the Jerusalem cult would have celebrated Yahweh's accession to the throne as king. To be sure, Hebrew grammar permits this translation. But it is exceedingly doubtful whether the Israelite faith, even in the cosmopolitan atmosphere of Jerusalem, adopted wholesale the ancient mythical views. The notion that Yahweh is involved in the cycles of the cosmos and must fight to win kingship anew at the turn of the year is completely alien to Israel's faith. "The gods of the peoples are idols," that is, natural powers within the cosmos, if not figments of human imagination, "but Yahweh made the heavens" (Ps. 96:5) and therefore transcends the whole cosmos. These psalms are explicit in saying that Yahweh's throne is established "from of old" (immeasurable past time), that Yahweh's kingdom is "from everlasting" (Ps. 93:2). Yahweh is the King who was, who is, and who is to come—to judge the earth with righteousness (Ps. 96:13). God who established the divine kingdom of old, and who will come in power to realize the divine rule with finality, is *now* enthroned on the praises of the people. The dimensions of time, expressed in the tenses of human experience, are expanded to their limit in the acclamation, "Yahweh is King!"

Nevertheless, it must be said that the kingship hymns celebrate an event, not a general truth. The translation of the cultic shout as "Yahweh reigns" may be too mild to do justice to the spirit of the Zion festival. The acclamation has a dynamic, eventful ring, something like the Easter hymn, "Jesus Christ is risen today, Alleluia!"

ENTHRONED OVER THE POWERS OF CHAOS

These psalms show how Israel appropriated the mythical imagery of the ancient world and converted it to the praise of Yahweh, the King of Israel and of the cosmos. The ancient myth of the Creator's victory over the powers of chaos, symbolized by "the deep," "the floods," "the sea," is used poetically to express the faith that no powers—whether historical enemies, evil, death, or anything else in creation—can subvert God's rule. In an ancient Israelite hymn, which displays the influence of Canaanite poetry, it is said:

Yahweh is enthroned above the flood,
Yahweh is enthroned as king forever.
—Psalm 29:10

This language also occurs in one of the hymns of Yahweh's kingship, where the poet portrays "the floods," "many waters," "the sea" lifting up their stormy waves, as though seeking to challenge the sovereignty of Yahweh. But the tumult is in vain, for Yahweh is enthroned transcendently.

The floods lift up, Yahweh,
the floods lift up their sound,
the floods lift up their pounding.
More majestic than the thunders of many waters,
more majestic than the breakers of the sea,
on high Yahweh is majestic!

—Psalm 93:3-4

As we have already seen in other psalms (e.g., Ps. 104), it is impossible to translate this poetic language into flat prose. The biblical poets express a human experience that is not confined to ancient Israel. There is disorder in the world which, from a human point of view, seems to challenge the sovereignty of God. The experience of the threat of chaos may be occasioned by the imminence of an invasion of a foe from the north, as in the case of Jeremiah's moving vision of the return of chaos (Jer. 4:23-26), or, in our own time, the ominous possibility of nuclear catastrophe. In the faith of the psalmists, however, God is enthroned triumphantly over the powers that threaten to plunge human history into meaningless disorder and chaos. As Creator, God stands beyond history, beyond the cosmos. Therefore Yahweh's kingship, celebrated in Zion, demonstrates firm divine control over the powers of chaos that threaten human existence. Notice that the poet extends a special invitation to "the sea," "the floods"—the remnant of chaos that potentially threatens the ordered world of creation—to join with nature and human beings in an anthem of praise:

Let the sea thunder and all that it holds,
and the world, with all who live in it;
let all the rivers clap their hands
and the mountains shout for joy,

at the presence of Yahweh, for he comes
to judge the earth,

to judge the world with righteousness
and the nations with strict justice.
        —Psalm 98:7-9 (JB);
        see also Ps. 96:10-13

Here the verb "judge" means much more than the English word suggests. It refers to the power to obtain and maintain justice and proper order—power which human rulers should have ("Give us a king to judge us," I Sam. 8:6) but which, in the biblical view, is vested supremely and ultimately in God.

The psalm just quoted shows that an important dimension of psalms of this type is their "eschatological outlook." In hymnic tones they express the expectation that the King is coming on the stage of history to consummate the divine rule. In the prophecy of Second Isaiah, this announcement was transposed into the key of the "good news" that later was heard in Jesus' preaching (Mark 1:15).

> How beautiful upon the mountains
>   are the feet of him who brings good tidings,
> who publishes peace, who brings good tidings of good,
>   who publishes salvation,
>   who says to Zion, "Your God reigns."
>   —Isaiah 52:7 (RSV)

Today the exclamation "The Lord is King" is raised hymnically in services of Christian worship. Indeed, in some Christian circles a feast has been celebrated in the autumn known as "The Feast of Christ the King." The Christian church reads the enthronement psalms in the context of the gospel, that, through Jesus Christ, God has inaugurated the divine kingdom by striking the decisive blow against all powers of oppression, darkness, chaos, and death. Those who celebrate Christ's kingship in the festivals of his enthronement are summoned to new action and responsibility in the world, whatever the odds may be, knowing that the decisive victory has already been won. We still live in a world where the weak are oppressed by the mighty, where the powers of chaos threaten to break over humanity, and where death imposes the final threat to the goodness and meaningfulness of life. Yet the Christian community, which celebrates God's triumph in Jesus Christ, also lives toward the final establishing of God's kingdom when, in accordance with the intention of the original creation, all human beings will become fully human and the non-human creation as well will participate in the consummation of God's creative and redemptive purpose (Rom. 8:19-23)—"a new heaven and a new earth." In the time between the advent of the King and the final establishment of the kingdom, Christians also pray the enthronement psalms in the spirit of the Lord's Prayer:

> *Thy kingdom come,*
> *thy will be done,*
> *on earth as it is in heaven.*
> *—Matthew 6:10*

THE PROMISES OF GRACE TO DAVID

We turn now from the theme of God's kingship to the related theme of the earthly king as the vicegerent of God, or, to use the more familiar language, God's "messiah." The Hebrew word for messiah *(mashiaḥ;* Greek, *christos)* literally means "anointed one," and in the period of early Israel was used of the reigning king. A good illustration is found in the story of David's flight from King Saul, in which at one point we are told that, when the opportunity presented itself, he declined to kill "Yahweh's anointed" (I Sam. 24:1-7; cf. 26:6-10). Eventually the term "messiah" came to be used of "the One who is to come" (Matt. 11:3; Luke 7:19-20). As we have seen previously (Chapter 1), the book of Psalms was finally edited and issued in the name of David, the royal prototype of the future messiah.

The rise of David as king and the selection of Jerusalem as the place of the central sanctuary had a far-reaching influence upon Israel's worship, and specifically upon the covenant festival celebrated in the Jerusalem Temple. Jerusalem theologians wanted to say that the rule of David was the climax of the sacred history which began with the migration of Abraham from Mesopotamia (Gen. 12:1-9) and which issued in the exodus from Egypt and the covenant at Sinai (Ex. 1-24). It was their conviction that, in raising up David to be king and in choosing Zion as the central sanctuary, Yahweh had led Israel into a new era which required a new theological understanding. This is the theme of Psalm 78, a storytelling psalm which we considered briefly in Chapter 2.

To understand this new kind of covenant theology which centered in David and Zion it is necessary to turn to the portion of the David story found in two important chapters: II Samuel 6 and 7. The first of these chapters relates that David, desiring to unify his kingdom on the basis of the religious loyalty of the tribal confederacy, brought the Ark of the Covenant—the portable "throne" on which Yahweh was thought to be invisibly enthroned in the midst of the people during their wars and wanderings—into his new capital of Jerusalem with the intention of housing it in a temple. Jerusalem was not to be just the city of David but "Zion, city of our God," the locus of Yahweh's real presence in the midst of the people. The last part of Psalm 24 is an ancient liturgy, possibly as old as the time of Solomon, which undoubtedly was used in reenacting the processional bearing of the Ark into the Jerusalem Temple where Yahweh was acclaimed as King. As the procession reaches the gates of Zion, voices sing antiphonally:

Gates, raise your arches,
  rise, you ancient doors,
Let the King of glory in!

  Who is this King of glory?
  Yahweh the strong, the valiant,
  Yahweh valiant in battle!
            —Psalm 24:7-8 (JB)

In the following verses the ritual is repeated and once
again the Divine Warrior, Yahweh, enthroned invisibly
on the Ark, is acclaimed as the glorious King.

Let us return for a moment to the story in II Samuel 6
and 7. David wanted to build Yahweh a "house" (temple),
comparable in magnificence to his own palace. The
prophet Nathan, however, opposed this plan and
delivered to the king an oracle in which Yahweh promised
David to build *him* a "house" (dynasty) which would
stand in perpetuity.

*Yahweh announces to you that Yahweh will make a "house"
for you:*

*When your days are completed and you rest with your
ancestors, I will raise up after you your offspring, who
will issue from your body, and I will stabilize his
kingdom.*

*He shall build a "house" for my name,
and I will establish his royal throne in perpetuity.
I will be Father to him, and he will be Son to me.*

*When he does wrong, I will chasten him with the rod of
human punishment,
    and with the stripes of human beings,
but my loyalty [ḥesed] I will not withdraw from him,
    as I did in the case of Saul, whom I removed before you.*

Before me your house and your kingdom will stand secure
perpetually,
your throne will be established in perpetuity.

—*II Samuel 7:11b-16*

This passage has been called "the magna carta of Old Testament messianism" (Roland Murphy). Notice that the Davidic covenant, unlike the Mosaic covenant, is not couched in conditional terms: "If you will obey my voice . . ." (Ex. 19:5-6). To be sure, it contains a conditional element in that wrong actions will have consequences that not even a king can escape. But God's relationship with the people, mediated through the reigning Davidic king, the "anointed one," is based solely on divine grace. Under no circumstance will Yahweh withdraw the covenant promise of loyalty [*hesed*] to David which is the basis of the stability of the kingdom and its indefinite duration. Fundamentally the covenant is unconditional—grounded on God's faithful promises and not upon the fallible actions of human beings or the contingencies of the future. This is an important theological line that leads into the New Testament, where the proclamation is made that God's relationship with people, mediated through Jesus, the Anointed One (Greek, *christos*, "Christ"), is grounded unconditionally in divine grace and that through Christ, God has ratified the promises of grace to Israel.

The fall festival in Jerusalem, then, acquired a special character owing to the celebration of the simultaneous founding of the Jerusalem sanctuary and the Davidic dynasty. According to this covenant theology, Yahweh is *the King* par excellence, as Isaiah perceived in his inaugural vision.

I saw Yahweh sitting upon a throne, high and lifted up; and his
train filled the temple.

—*Isaiah 6:1*

The King, whose throne is in heaven (Ps. 11:4), has chosen Zion as the center of the divine rule on earth and has chosen the Davidic king as the representative of the kingship of God in Israel.

Several psalms express this theological understanding of God's relationship to the people.

Psalm 78*   *A recitation of Yahweh's great deeds*

This psalm (see Chapter 2) contains a long summary of Yahweh's historical deeds, beginning with the exodus (vs. 1-66). It is particularly interesting, because the psalmist affirms that the old sacred history has come to an end, owing to the unfaithfulness of North Israel ("the tent of Joseph"). Yahweh has made a new beginning in history by raising up David to be king and by selecting Zion as the central sanctuary (vs. 67-72).

Psalm 132*   *A liturgy commemorating Yahweh's choice of David and of Zion*

Here the story in II Samuel 7 is clearly in mind. The psalm begins by recalling David's intention to build a sanctuary for Yahweh (vs. 1-5). It continues with a ritual that was undoubtedly used during the processional bearing of the Ark into the Jerusalem Temple (vs. 6-10). Recalling the ancient Song of the Ark (Num. 10:35-36), worshipers affirm that Yahweh has found a new dwelling place in Zion.

Arise, Yahweh, and go to your resting place,
You and the ark of your power!
Let your priests be vested in righteousness,
and let your devotees sing for joy!
—Psalm 132:8-9

The psalm concludes (vs. 11-18) with a reaffirmation of Yahweh's covenant with David and Yahweh's choice of Zion as the earthly center of the divine presence.

Psalm 89*   *A hymn and a lament based on Yahweh's covenant with David*

The first part of this psalm (vs. 1-37) is a hymn that praises Yahweh for the faithfulness *(ḥesed)* manifested in the covenant with David. The hymn echoes the covenant theology of II Samuel 7 and, in addition, strikes the note that Yahweh's power as Creator upholds the stability and continuity of the Davidic throne. The second part of the psalm is a lament (vs. 38-51) in which the psalmist complains that Yahweh apparently has forsaken the covenant with David, as evidenced by the defeat of the king in battle. He appeals to Yahweh to remove the calamity and thus to reaffirm the covenant loyalty once sworn to David.

[See also II Samuel 23:17, an old poem often called "the last words of David." Here the theme is the "covenant in perpetuity" *(berith 'olam)* that Yahweh has made with David and the resulting security and welfare of the Davidic rule. In this hymnic passage David is called, according to some translations, "the sweet psalmist of Israel" (RSV), though the meaning may be that David is "the favorite of the songs of Israel" (RSV margin).]

THE ANOINTED ONE

This Davidic covenant theology, with its twofold emphasis upon the choosing of David and the choosing of Zion, casts light on two groups of psalms in the Psalter: the royal psalms and the psalms of Zion.

The first group consists of those psalms in which the king is the central figure.

✓ *2 "You are my son, today I have begotten you"
  [A coronation psalm]

*18 "With the loyal thou dost show thyself loyal"
  [Thanksgiving for the king's victory]

20 "May we shout for joy over your victory!"
  [Prayer for the king's victory]

21 "In thy strength the king rejoices"
  [Coronation psalm]

45 "Your divine throne endures for ever"
  [Ode for a royal wedding]

72 "Give the king thy justice, O God"
  [Coronation psalm]

101 "I will sing of loyalty and of justice"
  [Coronation psalm]

✓*110 "The order of Melchizedek"
  [Coronation psalm]

144: "Rescue me from the many waters"
1-11 [Royal lament]

Captions are from the RSV.

Israel lived in an environment in which the king's authority was based upon a mythology that made him the representative and mediator of the divine order of the cosmos. An ancient Sumerian text traces kingship to a divine origin in primeval times, "when kingship was lowered from heaven."[7] The king, by virtue of his royal office, was elevated to a lofty status in society and, indeed, in God's cosmic administration. In ancient Babylonia the king was regarded as divinely commissioned; in Egypt, the Pharaoh was considered to be the divine Son of God. *Ex officio* the king was held to be the channel of cosmic blessing to the social order. He was the representative of his subjects before God, and the representative of God (or gods) to human beings.

In the royal psalms of the Psalter the king is extolled in the extravagant "court style" of the ancient Near East. He is called "the fairest of human beings" (Ps. 45:2); his rule is the source of divine blessing in society (Ps. 72:17); he is victorious over the powers of chaos symbolized by "the sea" and "the rivers" (Ps. 89:25); he is exalted to Yahweh's throne, where he sits at "the right hand of God" (Ps. 110:1). According to some translations of the royal wedding ode, Psalm 45, he is addressed as "God."

Your throne, O God,
stands for ever.
—Psalm 45:7 (NAB)

> [This translation is also given in the Jerusalem Bible and in the margin of the Revised Standard Version. In this sense the passage is quoted from the Greek translation (Septuagint) in the New Testament at one place: Hebrews 1:8. Some modern translations gloss over the problem by translating "your divine throne" (e.g., RSV). Even if the more difficult reading of the Hebrew is adopted, this isolated text provides no basis for the notion that in ancient Israel the king was regarded as divine.]

Israel, however, did not adopt the mythical view of the king without modification. According to Israelite tradition, kingship emerged not in mythical times but out of the harsh realities of secular politics, particularly the crisis caused by the Philistine attempt to build an empire in Palestine. Above all, the institution of kingship in Israel was connected with Israel's sacred history, that is, the formation of Israel as the People of God. The raising up of David was a decisive act of Yahweh in Israel's historical pilgrimage. Therefore, the royal psalms, despite their dependence upon the court poetry of the ancient world, do not confer divinity upon the king. The king is God's "Son" by adoption, as we read clearly in Psalm 2:7 (quoted in Acts 13:33).

This view, of course, reflects the theology of Nathan's oracle to David, discussed above. A special relationship exists between God and king ("I will be his father, and he shall be my son," II Sam. 7:14)—a relationship based on divine choice or adoption. This view is elaborated in Psalm 89, for instance, in these lines:

He will invoke me, "My father,
  my God and rock of my safety,"
and I shall make him my first-born,
  the Most High for kings on earth.
        —Psalm 89:26-27 (JB)

In short, the king's authority is not absolute: it is derived from Yahweh, who is *the* King. The Davidic king is *chosen* to perform a task: to rule as Yahweh's representative in the kingdom on earth. In this royal capacity, his role is to obtain justice for the weak and the oppressed and to mediate divine blessing to the social order (Ps. 72). Above all, the king rules under the judgment of God (cf. Deut. 17:14-20).

THE SON OF GOD

Let us focus our attention on a couple of royal psalms that portray the king as being elevated to a high position in God's cosmic administration.

In Psalm 2, quoted several times in the New Testament (see Appendix C), the king is designated "Son of God." The psalm was originally composed to celebrate the coronation of an Israelite king, at which time his divine "election," or adoption, was announced.

In the judgment of some scholars, the psalm reflects a ritual of coronation known in the ancient world, particularly in Egypt.[8] The king was crowned in the sanctuary, where he received the decree from God that made his rule legitimate. After the coronation, he ascended the throne and issued an ultimatum to his enemies. Couriers then ran to the surrounding districts, announcing that "so and so has become king!" and the people rejoiced, for his reign was regarded as the beginning of a new era of blessing for society and even for the natural realm (see Ps. 72:15-17).

Notice how the structure of Psalm 2 seems to accord with such a coronation ceremony.

    A.   Preparation (Ps. 2:1-3)
        The psalm begins with a portrayal of the rebellion of the nations against Yahweh's "anointed" (messiah, or reigning king). In antiquity a change of throne was the signal for revolutionary forces to break loose.

    B.   Installation (Ps. 2:4-6)
        Next, the announcement is made of Yahweh's installation of the king in the sanctuary, the "holy hill" of Zion.

    C.   Legitimation (Ps. 2:7-9)
        Then "the decree" of Yahweh—the protocol which endows the king with authority—is announced: the king is declared to be Yahweh's son, "begotten this day" (the day of coronation) and elected to universal rule.

    D.   Ultimatum (Ps. 2:10-11)
        Finally, the king issues his ultimatum: rebellious rulers and territories are warned to recognize his authority.

AT THE RIGHT HAND OF GOD

Psalm 110 also seems to reflect a coronation ceremony. The Hebrew text has suffered in transmission, which may indicate that the psalm is very old, reaching back into the period of the early monarchy. At one point the poet makes use of the ancient tradition about Melchizedek, a Canaanite priest-king of the pre-Israelite city of Jerusalem (Salem). According to the tradition found in an unusual chapter in the book of Genesis, ch. 14, this priest-king of the ancient Canaanite city-state blessed Abraham in the name of the Canaanite god, 'El 'Elyon, "God Most High," who is acclaimed as "maker of heaven and earth" (Gen. 14:17-20).

Building on this curious tradition, the psalm begins with an oracle (Ps. 110:1), presumably given in the sanctuary, in which the officiating priest addresses the king as "my lord," a royal title. According to the oracle, Yahweh invites the king to sit on Yahweh's throne—at Yahweh's right hand! This is an astounding idea—that a king should, as it were, sit beside God, sharing the throne of God.

[Once the psalm was taken out of a coronation setting, the language concerning Yahweh (Adonai, translated "the Lord") and "my lord" (the king) was taken in a new way. In the postexilic period, when there were no kings on the throne of Judah and when David was regarded as the author of the psalm, it was construed, somewhat freely, to mean that David addressed the coming messiah as "my lord." In this sense ("The Lord said to my Lord") the verse is interpreted messianically in the New Testament, e.g., Mark 12:36. See Appendix C.]

The remainder of the psalm portrays the exaltation of the king to the highest position of honor. Speaking in the name of Yahweh, the priest first announces that from Zion the power of the king will extend throughout the nation and beyond (Ps. 110:2-3). Then he sets forth the divine oath by which the king is legitimated as priest-king in the succession of Melchizedek, who had both political and religious authority (110:4). Finally (110:5-7), he gives the assurance that the Lord (Yahweh) will be at the king's right hand (here the idiom differs from "the right hand" in v. 1). This means that Yahweh will ever be near the king to help in overthrowing hostile powers.

In using this hyperbolic language, found in both coronation psalms (Ps. 2 and 110), Israelite court poets have glorified the office of the king far beyond the political realities of the modest Davidic monarchy. At no time did Davidic kings achieve the universal sway promised in the coronation ritual. The portrayal of the king does not conform to any specific king of the house of David, not even David himself. Rather, it depicts the *type* of the true king who perfectly combines power and goodness—a historically rare, if not impossible, combination! Since the type was not perfectly embodied in any of the Davidic kings, it is understandable that in the course of time, especially after the collapse of the Davidic monarchy in 587 B.C., these psalms were interpreted to refer to *the* "Anointed One" (Messiah) of the future, who would come in the fullness of time to rule over God's kingdom on earth.

Thus the extravagant language of the royal psalms, which was once court flattery, came to be understood as pointing to *the* king, *the* messiah, of the future. The distinguished Old Testament theologian, Gerhard von Rad, once observed that we really do not know whether those who paid homage to the king in this extravagant manner were filled with doubt about him and were asking in their hearts, as did John the Baptist later, "Are you he who is to come, or shall we look for another?"[9] (Matt. 11:3). In any case, the royal psalms were retained and used in worship long after kingship had become a thing of the past in Israel's history. It is significant that in the postmonarchic period, when the final revision of the Psalter was issued, the songs (psalms) of Israel were attributed to David. The people regarded David as the type of the true king, who represented them before God and who mediated God's kingly rule on earth. They prayed the psalms "in David," so to speak. The New Testament shows that early Christians prayed the psalms "in Christ"—the Anointed One *(christos)* who belongs in David's lineage but who far exceeds the Davidic type.

THE CITY OF GOD

Several psalms are often grouped under the rubric of "songs of Zion," for they express the view that Yahweh has chosen Zion as the earthly center of the divine rule. The title itself is taken from Ps. 137, which voices the despondency of people uprooted from their homeland and taken into Babylonian exile. Their captors taunted them, doubtless saying, "Where is your God?" (Lam. 2:15; Ps. 79:10; cf. Ps. 42:3, 10), and demanded that they sing "one of the songs of Zion."

How could we sing
one of Yahweh's hymns
in a pagan country?
Jerusalem, if I forget you,
may my right hand wither!

May I never speak again,
if I forget you!
If I do not count Jerusalem
the greatest of my joys!
—Psalm 137:4-6 (JB)

The title, although actually drawn from a lament, is quite appropriate for the psalms we are about to consider, whose mood of exultation stands out all the more sharply by contrast with that of exiles who wept over the destruction of the Temple at Jerusalem.

SONGS OF ZION

*46 "God is our refuge and strength"
 48 "The city of the great King"
 76 "His dwelling place in Zion"
*84 "How lovely is thy dwelling place"
 87 "Glorious things are spoken of you"
*121 "I lift up my eyes to the hills"
*122 "Pray for the peace of Jerusalem"

Captions are from the RSV.

The songs of Zion presuppose a major tenet of Davidic covenant theology: Yahweh has chosen Zion as the place of the divine presence (see Ps. 132:13-18). Just as Israel's poets spoke of the Davidic king in extravagant court language, so Zion was glorified in poetic language that has mythical overtones. The holy mountain, "beautiful in elevation" and "the joy of all the earth" (Ps. 48:2), was identified with Mt. Casius (Mt. Zaphon) in Syria, the Olympus of the north which Canaanites regarded as the dwelling place of the gods. According to poetic vision, the Temple was situated at the "navel," or center, of the universe, where heaven and earth meet; and from a source beneath the Temple a life-giving stream sprang up ("the river of God," Ps. 46:4) and flowed from the city to the Dead Sea, transforming the wilderness into a fertile region and converting the Dead Sea into a freshwater lake (Ezek. 47:1-12; cf. Rev. 22:1-2). In a priestly passage of the Pentateuch there is a suggestion that the sanctuary in Jerusalem was constructed according to a heavenly model (Ex. 25:9), just as Babylonian temples were regarded as miniature replicas of a heavenly prototype.[10]

This mythical language is used, of course, for poetic adornment. The mythical view of the temples of the ancient Near East has been modified. In the Israelite view, Zion was not a holy hill from primeval times; rather, at a particular point in history, in the time of David, it became sacred, the place where Yahweh chose to be present in the midst of the people. Hence, it came to be the sanctuary to which the people made their pilgrimages.

In our age of universalism this emphasis upon the centrality of Zion is hard to understand. It sounds a bit nationalistic and theologically offensive. Surely, if God is present at all in the midst of the people, the divine presence could be celebrated in one place as well as in another. Why should Zion receive theological priority over sanctuaries in Rome, Canterbury, New York, or elsewhere? The answer is that Zion has come to be a symbol whose meaning transcends the politics of David or the geography of Palestine. The Zion psalms express an ecumenicity that arises out of historical rootedness and particularity. To the psalmists, Zion was the center of historical meaning which God had disclosed to Israel and, *through* Israel, to the whole world. The meaning unveiled in Israel's history is not confined to Israel; it is the meaning of all human existence with its history of wars, animosities, and misunderstandings—the history portrayed in the story of the Tower of Babel (Gen. 11:1-9). In a passage about the "last days"—the consummation of history—it is announced that ultimately all nations and peoples will make a pilgrimage to Zion.

In the days to come
the mountain of the Temple of Yahweh
shall tower above the mountains
*   and be lifted higher than the hills.*
All the nations will stream to it,
*   peoples without number will come to it;*
*   and they will say:*
*   "Come, let us go up to the mountain of Yahweh,*
*   to the Temple of the God of Jacob*

that he may teach us his ways
so that we may walk in his paths;
since the Law [torah] will go out from Zion,
and the oracle of Yahweh from Jerusalem."

He will wield authority over the nations
and adjudicate between many peoples;
these will hammer their swords into ploughshares,
their spears into sickles.
Nation will not lift sword against nation,
there will be no more training for war.
                              —*Isaiah 2:2-4 (JB)*

The Christian faith, with its spacious universalism, does not surrender the centrality of Zion. The whole drama of God's dealings with the people leads up to the appearance of the Messiah in Jerusalem, and to his death and victory there—the crucial event which is reenacted in Christian worship. Zion is the historical center around which is gathered the people of God, whose membership is determined by God's choosing, not by human standards. It is theologically appropriate, then, that Psalm 87:3 became the text of Augustine's monumental work *The City of God*. Centuries later, the same text inspired the composition of the hymn by John Newton (1725-1807), "Glorious Things of Thee Are Spoken, Zion, City of Our God."

PILGRIM PSALMS

In view of what has been said, it is understandable that some psalms express an intense longing to make a pilgrimage to the Temple of Jerusalem. This longing, as we have noticed at the beginning of this chapter, could be expressed in a lament on the part of a person who could not join the procession (Ps. 42-43); but it could also be expressed in joyful anticipation by pilgrims on their way to Jerusalem.

The Psalter now includes one collection of psalms known as "psalms of ascents" (Ps. 120-134). In at least two of these psalms, Psalms 120 and 121, this title refers to festival caravans that enabled pilgrims to go up to "the hill of Yahweh." Foot travel was difficult in those days, but pilgrims took confidence in the protecting care of Yahweh, "your shade on your right hand" (Ps. 121:5). After many experiences along the way, people rejoiced to be standing at last within the gates of Jerusalem and were glad that they had responded positively to the invitation to join the pilgrimage.

How I rejoiced when they said to me,
"Let us go to the house of Yahweh!"
And now our feet are standing
in your gateways, Jerusalem.
—Psalm 122:1-2 (JB)

We should not suppose the psalmists believed that God was present in the Temple in the sense that the earthly temple was literally the divine dwelling. In various ways the interpreters of Israel's faith have sought to do justice to the paradox that the Holy God, who is not part of our human world, becomes present to the people in worship. In Solomon's prayer, associated with the dedication of the Jerusalem Temple, the speaker exclaims: "Heaven and the highest heaven cannot contain thee [God]; how much less this house" built by human hands (I Kings 8:27)! The problem of the "transcendence" and "immanence" of God, to use philosophical language, was dealt with by saying that Yahweh, the Holy God, causes the divine name to be in the sanctuary. The name, according to the view that prevails in the book of Deuteronomy and material edited from a Deuteronomic point of view, is Yahweh's alter ego, or "other self." The name of God can be invoked in the sanctuary without God becoming localized there.

One of the most beautiful songs of Zion is Psalm 84, a pilgrimage psalm in which a poet envies the birds that find security in the Temple structure and exclaims that even one day spent in the Temple courts is better than a thousand spent elsewhere.

How lovely is your tabernacle,
  O Yahweh of hosts!
My whole being longs and yearns
  for Yahweh's [Temple] courts.
My heart and my flesh sing for joy
  to the living God.

Even the sparrow finds a home,
  and the swallow a nest
in which she lays her young—
right at your altars, O Yahweh of hosts,
my King and my God.
                                    —Psalm 84:1-3

Here we seem to have another view of God's real presence in the midst of the people. The central sanctuary is described as the "dwelling place" or, as rendered in some translations, the "tabernacle" (*mishkanoth*, the Hebrew word is in plural). This may reflect the ancient tradition that Yahweh "tents" or "goes about" among the people (cf. Lev. 26:11-13).[11] In this view, the Temple is not Yahweh's "home," as though Yahweh dwelt or resided there, but the place of divine visitation from time to time.

In this sense, the psalmist—probably on a pilgrimage to Jerusalem—anticipates the "tabernacling presence" of God in the Temple as the people invoke the name of Yahweh and engage in the drama of worship. Strikingly, the psalmist says that "the God of gods will be seen in Zion" (Ps. 84:7)—perhaps a reference to dramatic ceremonies such as the Ark procession. Both auditory and visual elements, hearing and seeing, song and sacramental rite, combine in the service of worship in which God chooses to become present, enthroned on the praises of the people.

OUR REFUGE AND STRENGTH

In the songs of Zion and many other psalms in the Psalter the Temple of Jerusalem is regarded as a bulwark of security precisely because it is the place where God is present in the midst of the people. In popular theology, the confidence in the Temple as a sanctuary of protection led to a false sense of security and to the notion that people can worship God and "get away with murder" and exploitation of the poor. In his "Temple sermon" (Jer. 7:1-15; see ch. 26), Jeremiah issued a strong condemnation of this popular "Temple theology."

Hear the word of Yahweh, all you of Judah who enter by these gates to worship Yahweh! . . .

"Reform the whole pattern of your conduct, so that I may dwell with you in this place. Do not put your trust in that lie: 'This is Yahweh's temple, Yahweh's temple, Yahweh's temple!' No! Only if you really reform your whole pattern of conduct—if you really behave justly one toward another, no longer oppress the alien, the orphan, and the widow [nor shed innocent blood in this place], nor follow other gods to your own hurt—only then can I dwell with you in this place, in the land that I gave to your fathers of old for all time to come."[12]

—Jeremiah 7:2-7

The "ifs" in this sermon indicate that Jeremiah, who stood in the tradition of Mosaic covenant theology with its conditional emphasis, was attacking the false confidence in the Temple engendered by Davidic theology.

[The translation of vs. 3 and 7 of the Temple sermon. "I [Yahweh] will dwell with you in this place," reflects the premise of Davidic theology that Yahweh elected Zion as the divine dwelling place; therefore, the Temple was a sanctuary of safety in the presence of God. Jeremiah attacks this view with the kind of theological emphasis reflected in Psalm 81; see the discussion above, pp. 196-197.]

However, the Temple theology associated with Zion cannot be dismissed on the basis of its popular misunderstanding or its misuse to justify a particular life-style. To appreciate Zion theology, one should turn to its best interpreters. In the prophetic tradition, one should turn to Isaiah of Jerusalem, who preceded Jeremiah by about a century. Standing firmly in the tradition of Davidic theology, with its twin convictions of Yahweh's election of the Davidic king and the election of Zion, this prophet announced that the presence of the Holy God in the midst of the people (Immanuel, "God with us") means a divine judgment that purifies Zion so that it may truly be the City of God (Isa. 1:21-26) and the raising up of a faithful king to sit upon the throne of David (Isa. 7:1-17; 9:2-7).[13]

In the Psalter the theme of Yahweh's dwelling in Zion receives its profoundest treatment in Psalm 46, one of the best-known psalms, thanks in part to Martin Luther, who found in the psalm the keynote for his hymn of the Reformation: "A Mighty Fortress Is Our God." In the spirit of Isaiah of Jerusalem, the psalmist glorifies Zion for the purpose of announcing that human confidence is grounded in the transcendent sovereignty of God, whose cosmic rule is known and celebrated in Zion.

The theme of confidence in the transcendent God, whose sovereignty over the cosmos and history is centered in Zion, is developed in three strophes. Each strophe is punctuated with the choral refrain:

Yahweh of hosts is with us,
the God of Jacob is our bulwark.

[This is, of course, the theme of Immanuel, "God with us," which was prominent in the message of Isaiah of Jerusalem (Isa. 7:14; 8:8) and indeed in Israelite worship in general (cf. Amos 5:14). The Immanuel ("God is with us") antiphonal refrain is heard in vs. 7 and 11 of the psalm in its present arrangement. However, from a stylistic point of view, it should also resound at the end of v. 3 at the point marked by *Selah*, possibly a term referring to a musical interlude. The threefold choral response is proposed in some modern translations (e.g., NAB and JB).]

In the first strophe (vs. 1-3 + refrain) the poet draws on mythical language to describe the shaking of the foundations of earthly existence. Even though the earth should be shaken with cosmic tumult and the waters of chaos were to threaten to overwhelm, God is the transcendent source of the meaning of human existence and the whole cosmos.

Therefore we will not fear though the earth should change,
though the mountains shake in the heart of the sea;
though its waters roar and foam,
though the mountains tremble with its tumult.
—Psalm 46:2-3 (RSV)

In the second strophe (vs. 4-6 + refrain) the poet also draws on mythical language to portray the transcendent meaning of Zion, "the city of God." Zion is portrayed as an Olympus (cf. Ps. 48:1), through which runs a marvelous river of God, welling up from the subterranean abyss. The life-giving river, which erupts at the center of the earth, signifies that God is "in the midst" of Zion. God is present "with us." Therefore, the people may trust that, even when they are threatened by conflict and catastrophe, divine help will come with the break of dawn.

The climactic third strophe (vs. 8-10 + refrain) opens with an invitation to worshipers to contemplate the awesome deeds of God in the earth (cf. Ps. 66:5). The "raging of the nations," referred to in the previous strophe, is now portrayed as feverish military preparations, perhaps for an assault on the citadel of Zion (as in Ps. 2:1-3).

Come, think of Yahweh's marvels,
   the astounding things he has done in the world;
   all over the world he puts an end to wars,
   he breaks the bow, he snaps the spear,
   he gives shields to the flames.
                    —Psalm 46:8-9 (JB)

Seen under the aspect of God's eternal sovereignty, the military activities of nations, who foolishly suppose that their power is decisive, are in vain. Above the tumult and shouting of history the community of faith hears the sovereign command of the God whose deity must finally be recognized.

The divine oracle ("Be still and know . . .") with which the strophe concludes has often been misunderstood as a summons to quiet meditation or a spiritual pause. However, the Hebrew imperative carries the strong meaning of "Desist!" (NAB, v. 11), "Give in!" (Moffatt), "Let be!" (NEB)—as in an authoritative command to contentious persons to "Shut up" or "Stop it!"

Yield, and acknowledge that I am God!
   I am exalted among the nations,
   exalted in the earth!
                    —Psalm 46:10

Powers that oppose God's will for *shalom* (peace, welfare) are summoned with a stentorian command to cease and desist, and to admit that God is in ultimate control of the affairs of human history.

Martin Luther's Reformation hymn, alluded to earlier,

has given the tones of Psalm 46 a new resonance. The hymn affirms that God is a bulwark against the prevailing "flood" of mortal ills; that we would be lost in the battle with dark and demonic forces if we trusted in our own resources; and that through Jesus Christ, God speaks the divine word "above all earthly powers."

NOTES

1. See Ch. 1, "The Cultic Element," in Helmer Ringgren, *The Faith of the Psalmists* (Fortress Press, 1963). He writes: "The psalms were not written for private use—at least, not originally, but for use in the cult of the Yahweh community, and in most cases the cult of the preexilic community" (p. 1).

2. Roland Murphy observes that "a liturgical mime" must have accompanied a poem such as Psalm 46; the invitation to "behold the works of the Lord" suggests that "some activity accompanied the poem" (*The Psalms, Job*, Proclamation Commentaries [Fortress Press, 1977], p. 13).

3. See Walter Harrelson, *Interpreting the Old Testament* (Holt, Rinehart & Winston, 1964), p. 122.

4. See *The Book of Worship* of The United Methodist Church.

5. Artur Weiser, *The Psalms, A Commentary*, trans. Herbert Hartwell, The Old Testament Library (Westminster Press, 1962).

6. Sigmund Mowinckel, *The Psalms in Israel's Worship*, trans. D. R. Ap-Thomas (Abingdon Press, 1962), Vol. 1.

7. The Sumerian king list, dating back to the third millennium B.C., is found in James B. Pritchard (ed.), *Ancient Near Eastern Texts Relating to the Old Testament* (Princeton University Press, 1969), p. 265.

8. See Gerhard von Rad, *Old Testament Theology*, Vol. 1, trans. D. M. G. Stalker (Harper & Row, 1962), pp. 318-320.

9. Ibid., p. 324.

10. See Mircea Eliade's discussion of "The Symbolism of the Center" in *Cosmos and History: The Myth of the Eternal Return*, trans. Willard R. Trask (Harper & Brothers, 1959), pp. 12-17.

11. See Frank M. Cross, "The Priestly Work," in *Canaanite Myth and Hebrew Epic* (Harvard University Press, 1973), p. 299.

12. Translation of Jer. 7:2-7 by John Bright, based on ancient versions, in *Jeremiah*, The Anchor Bible (Doubleday & Co., 1965), p. 52.

13. See further Bernhard W. Anderson, *The Eighth Century Prophets: Amos, Hosea, Isaiah, Micah*, Proclamation Commentaries (Fortress Press, 1978), Ch. 6.

7
LIKE A TREE
PLANTED BY WATERS

Many of the psalms, as we have seen, presuppose the setting of a people gathered for worship on holy days or on high holy days of religious festivals, such as the New Year. Even today these psalms are used cultically as the people of God raise their praises in the forms of lament (petition), songs of thanksgiving, and hymnic doxologies. But the psalms cannot be confined to cultic use. This is clear when one considers that the Psalter, in its final form, was not just a hymnbook intended for use in the Temple of Jerusalem. The editors of this collection also had in mind the use of the psalms for religious education and spiritual sustenance—as is evident from the position at the beginning of the Psalter of two psalms, one dealing with the study of the Torah (law) and the other with the Messiah (Ps. 1 and 2). With these psalms the editors invited their readers "to choose the right path to the Messianic glory: the study of the law and the obedience toward the word of God."[1]

The final adaptation of the Psalter for use in instruction as well as in worship took place during the period following the return from Babylonian exile in the sixth century B.C. At this time a new form of gathering—possibly related to the situation of worship in exile—gained importance in the Israelite community and eventually developed into the assembly known as the synagogue.

Even after the Temple at Jerusalem was rebuilt, the people found that more and more their life centered in the kind of gathering that provided occasions for prayer and edification. In this new community setting, many psalms became detached from their original cultic situations in Temple worship and were read simply as "spiritual songs"—affirmations of trust, expressions of delight in the Torah, and "wisdom" meditations upon the problems of existence. The new style of synagogue worship had a profound influence upon the early Christian community which was also concerned with "the right path to the Messianic glory."

SPIRITUAL SONGS

Previously we have noticed that the type of psalm called a lament moves quickly from a cry out of distress toward an expression of trust in God. Frequently this note of confidence is introduced by a conjunction (in Hebrew) which is translated by an adversative: "but," "yet," "nevertheless." *In spite of* affliction, the psalmist affirms faith in Yahweh. For example:[2]

But I put my trust in you, Yahweh,
 I say, "You are my God."
My times are in your hand.
                    —Psalm 31:14-15a

There are a number of psalms, however, in which the motif of trust is developed as a self-contained song. These "songs of trust" have been plausibly explained as an independent development of the confession of trust which is a characteristic feature of the lament. They provide evidence of the way in which an important element of a psalm could become detached from a cultic form and setting and, with freedom of its own, come to be "a spiritual song."

SONGS OF TRUST

11 "If the foundations are destroyed"
16 "In thy presence there is fulness of joy"
*23 "My cup overflows"
*27:
1-6 "He will set me high upon a rock"
       [The second part of the psalm is a lament]
62 "For God alone my soul waits in silence"
*63 "Thy steadfast love is better than life"
*91 "My refuge and my fortress"
*121 "I lift up my eyes to the hills"
       [Also classified as a pilgrimage psalm]
125 "Like Mount Zion, which cannot be moved"
131 "Like a child that is quieted is my soul"

Captions are from the RSV.

[Psalm 4 is sometimes classified as a song of trust rather than an individual lament. In this list, Psalm 63 may be regarded as an individual lament, and Psalm 125 may be considered a community lament. The line between the two types—the lament and the song of trust—often cannot be drawn sharply.]

In these psalms of trust we find various references to cultic actions such as the offering of sacrifices (Ps. 4:5), singing and dancing before Yahweh, or sojourning (dwelling) in Yahweh's "tent" (Ps. 27:4-6). The question may be raised, however, as to whether this traditional language, which was originally associated with worship services, came to be "spiritually interpreted" (Eissfeldt), that is, whether the language is now metaphorical. Certainly the primary concern of the psalmists is the sense of the nearness and saving power of God, which the people once experienced in the Temple cult. In a later period, when the Temple cult had lost its centrality for many people, "the concrete experience of the nearness of

God in the Temple" as Artur Weiser observes, was "expanded and deepened"[3] and thus the old language was interpreted symbolically. This emancipation of the language of the psalms from the sphere of worship in the Jerusalem Temple took place, as we have already noted, during the postexilic period when the synagogue began to occupy an important place in the life of the people. And this development, in turn, paved the way for the time when Jesus proclaimed that God is not to be worshiped exclusively in any geographical sphere, whether in Shechem (as the Samaritans advocated) or in Jerusalem (as the Jews claimed); rather, "the true worshipers will worship the Father in spirit and truth" (John 4:23-24).

THE SHEPHERD'S PSALM

As an illustration of the songs of trust, we turn to the well-known Twenty-third Psalm. By virtue of its profound simplicity and matchless beauty this psalm has touched the hearts of countless people down through the centuries. Here is a poem that children have learned by heart, that has sustained the mature in the perplexities of life, and that has been a peaceful benediction on the lips of the dying. No single psalm has expressed more powerfully many people's prayer of confidence "out of the depths" to the God whose purpose alone gives meaning to the span of life, from womb to tomb. Since the Twenty-third Psalm is so familiar, especially in the classical King James Version, it may be well to read it in a fresh translation.

Yahweh is my Shepherd, nothing do I lack.
In grassy meadows you make me repose,
By restful waters* you lead me.

---

*The poet refers to watering places where sheep find security and refreshment.

You revive my whole being!
You guide me into the right paths for your name's sake.
Even when I go through the valley of deep darkness,
I fear nothing sinister;
for you are at my side!
Your rod and staff reassure me.

You spread out before me a table,
in sight of those who threaten me.
You pour upon my head festive oil.
My cup is brimming over!
Certainly, divine goodness and grace attend me throughout
all my days,
and I shall be a guest in Yahweh's house as long as I live.

—Psalm 23

[After the thematic sentence found in v. 1, verses 2 and 3 are translated in the second person singular in agreement with the personal address in vs. 4-5. In the last verse the translation follows some versions that read "and I dwell," rather than the received Hebrew text, "and I return." Here the idea is not that of taking up residence permanently in the Temple, but rather, as in Ps. 15:1, being a guest or sojourner in Yahweh's "tent"—that is, frequently visiting the Temple, where God is present. In v. 4 the author has adopted the translation "they assure me" from the Jewish scholar, Julius Morgenstern. On oil as a symbol of festive joy (v. 5), see Ps. 45:7; 92:10-11; 133:2.]

The major problem in interpreting this psalm is that it presents two images that are quite different. In vs. 1-4, Yahweh is portrayed as the good Shepherd who cares for the flock; in vs. 5 and 6, on the other hand, Yahweh is the Host who offers hospitality to a guest and protects the guest from enemies. In German it can be said, with a euphonious play on words, that Yahweh is *mein Hirt und mein Wirt* ("my Shepherd and my Host"), but in the poem itself the images do not seem to harmonize so nicely. What do the shepherd and the host really have to do with each other?

This problem begins to resolve itself when we project ourselves imaginatively out of our industrial milieu into the pastoral way of life which still prevails in some parts of the world today. The shepherd can be portrayed from two standpoints. He is the protector of the sheep as they wander in search of grazing land. Yet he is also the protector of the traveler who finds hospitality in his tent from the dangers and enemies of the desert.[4] Even today the visitor to certain parts of the Middle East can see the scene that lies at the basis of the psalm: the black camel's hair tent where the traveler receives Bedouin hospitality, and the surrounding pastureland where the sheep graze under the protection of the shepherd. In Psalm 23, Yahweh is portrayed as the Shepherd in both aspects of the shepherd's life: as the Leader of the flock, and as the hospitable Host.

In the first part of the psalm, the psalmist likens personal trust in Yahweh to that of sheep who confidently follow the shepherd as he leads them to green pastures and by quiet waters. This image is found repeatedly in the Old Testament (Ps. 80:1; 95:7; 100:3; Isa. 40:11; 49:9f.; 63:14; Ezek. 34:10ff.). It is recapitulated in the New Testament in the parable of the lost sheep (Luke 15:3-7) and in the Johannine picture of Jesus Christ as the good Shepherd (John 10:1-18). The image is admirably suited to express the understanding that human beings are not the ultimate measure of things, the controller of their world, or the determiner of their destiny. Yahweh, the psalmist affirms, is Israel's Maker; therefore the people belong to Yahweh, depending upon their God as sheep are related to their shepherd (see Ps. 95:6-7; 100:3). Of course, the image of the shepherd and his flock should not be understood merely in an idyllic sense. In the ancient Near East the king was regarded as the shepherd of his people.

To address Yahweh as Shepherd was to acknowledge that Yahweh rules with kingly power.

Here is the Lord Yahweh coming with power,
his arm subduing all things to him.
The prize of his victory is with him,
his trophies all go before him.
He is like a shepherd feeding his flock,
gathering lambs in his arms,
holding them against his breast
and leading to their rest the mother ewes.
—*Isaiah 40:10-11 (JB)*

This confidence that Yahweh is Israel's shepherd, which the psalmist personally appropriates by saying "my shepherd," leads immediately to the affirmation that nothing more is needful—a statement that sounds somewhat strange in our commercialized world where the media of communication conspire to prove how much we are lacking. The psalmist's thought is echoed in many other psalms—for example, the testimony that those who trust Yahweh "lack no good thing" (Ps. 34:8-10) or that Yahweh is one's "portion constantly" even though physical energies ebb (Ps. 73:25-26).

Having gone this far into the psalm, we now need to consider something that may have escaped attention: the psalm has a superscription which associates it with David, "the shepherd of Israel." In the introductory chapter it was said that this title *(leDawid)* is ambiguous: it may mean "to David" (in dedication), "of David" (belonging to David), or "for David" (to be used by the Davidic king in worship). This problem is resolved in the final form of the Psalter, in which David is presented as the ideal king ("anointed one," messiah) who "speaks for" the people in expressing their faith in God.

In this representative role the Davidic king does not espouse a fainthearted, otherworldly faith which turns away from the experiences of this life and seeks fulfillment in some higher realm. On the contrary, he testifies that his faith in God has repeatedly renewed his life at the very core of his being (the Hebrew *nefesh*, often translated "soul" at v. 3a, really means "my self," "my being"). He discerns a meaning flowing through his life, which he can account for only by saying that Yahweh, like a shepherd who guides his sheep into the right trails (the trails that are beneficial for the flock), has been directing his life along a course that leads toward fulfillment. The psalmist is aware of the threats to his existence (cf. Ps. 5:8); but even more, he is aware of God's saving action bestowed only for the sake of his divine honor, that is, because God's nature (name) is gracious. (See the discussion of God's name, Chapter 5.) Just as the sheep do not always pasture in verdant meadows or drink at quiet waters but at times must walk precariously through the dark and narrow valley where wild beasts and other dangers lurk, so the psalmist affirms that God has guided him through experiences that put him under trial or brought him to the point of death. The familiar translation "the shadow of death" goes beyond the meaning of the Hebrew term, which means "deep darkness" (Amos 5:8; Isa. 9:2; Ps. 44:19). Yet this secondary interpretation is consistent with the original meaning, for in the view of the psalmists the power of death encroaches into a person's life when the vitality of bodily life is weakened. (See the discussion of death in Chapter 4.)

In the second part of the psalm (vs. 5-6) the imagery shifts to the shepherd as host. According to the Bedouin law of hospitality, once a traveler is received into the shepherd's tent, and especially once his host has spread food before him, he is guaranteed immunity from enemies who may be attempting to overtake him. In pastoral circles no human protection is greater than that afforded by the hospitality of a Bedouin chief. So the psalmist expresses trust in the good Shepherd by saying that in Yahweh's tent one finds a protecting and gracious welcome. This divine hospitality is not just a temporary reprieve but a limitless protection from the powers that threaten one's existence. The Host's tent is none other than the Temple, as in Psalm 27:1-6 which closely parallels the thought of Psalm 23.

For he will hide me in his shelter
  in the day of trouble;
he will conceal me under the cover of his tent,
  he will set me high upon a rock.
Psalm 27:5 (RSV); cf. Ps. 61:4

The psalmist declares that in Yahweh's house ("tent") a table is prepared before him (perhaps a reference to a sacrificial meal in the Temple; Ps. 22:26) and he is given the most cordial welcome—right in sight of his enemies. (See Ps. 27:6, and the discussion of the enemies, Chapter 3.) Now it is no longer his enemies who "pursue" him; rather, it is Yahweh's grace and goodness that follow after him as long as he lives.

Some commentators have suggested that the Shepherd's Psalm was composed by a person who in the maturity of life looked back across the years and traced the purpose of God through the whole story. One commentator writes:

The sentiments of an almost childlike trust which the poet is able to express in this psalm are, however, by no means the product of a carefree unconcern characteristic of young people; on the contrary, they are the mature fruit of a heart which, having passed through many bitter experiences and having fought many battles (vv. 4, 5), had been allowed to find at the decline of life in its intimate communion with God (vv. 2, 6) the serenity of a contented spirit—peace of mind (v. 6) and, in all dangers, strength.[5]

Perhaps it is fair to deduce this much from the psalm. In any case, the language has spoken to many people with increasing depth of meaning through the maturing years which hasten toward the "deep darkness." And when the psalm is read from the standpoint of Christian faith, it speaks of a table graciously spread, not only in the presence of the hostile powers of this age but also in the presence of "the last enemy" (I Cor. 15:26).

THE PROTECTING SHADOW

Trust in Yahweh finds its most powerful, and at the same time most problematic, expression in Psalm 91, another well-known song of trust. The psalm, however, is difficult to interpret. The difficulty arises in part from the question of how to understand the overall structure of the psalm and its three component parts. Who is the speaker and the one spoken to? What setting in worship is reflected? How does the climactic divine oracle (vs. 14-16) relate to the previous parts? Since these questions cannot be answered decisively, the psalm presents a challenge to the interpreter.

A. Refuge in God (Ps. 91:1-2)
    In the introduction someone addresses a person who seeks shelter in the protecting care of God symbolized by the Temple (Ps. 27:5; 61:4). Possibly the psalmist has in mind the ancient view that a holy place was an asylum in which fugitives could find refuge ("sanctuary") from the hasty justice of their pursuers by grasping "the horns of the altar" (see I Kings 1:50-51). The asylum motif is suggested by the language in v. 1 and especially later in v. 4, where the poet refers to protection beneath the outspread wings of the Cherubim in the Holy of Holies of the Temple. This ancient

custom, as well as the location of the sacred Ark in the Temple, now provides the metaphorical imagery that enlarges the horizon of thought beyond the limitations of time and place. Any person within the community of faith may be addressed. Notice that epithets for deity, inherited from the pre-Israelitic environment, are mentioned first: 'Elyon, translated as "the Most High," and Shaddai, translated as "the Almighty"; but these terms are subordinated to the worshiper's relationship to God known by the personal name Yahweh.

Whoever dwells in the shelter of Elyon,
  and tarries in the shadow of Shaddai,
will say to Yahweh:
  "My refuge and my fortress,
My God in whom I trust!"
               —Psalm 91:1-2

  B. Instruction in Faith (Ps. 91:3-13)
     In the next section the person addressed is informed about what trusting Yahweh will mean in the stresses and strains of daily life. The identity of the speaker is not disclosed. Is it a priest who gives *torah* (instruction)? Is it a wisdom teacher who sets forth a traditional philosophy of life found, for instance, on the lips of one of Job's "pastoral counselors" (Job 5:17-27)? Or is it an ordinary person who "teaches" others out of the experience of help received from Yahweh?[6] In any case, the speaker sets forth a rather elementary view of God's protecting presence—a view that is unqualified by exceptions to glittering generalities, untouched by any notion that suffering may

be divine discipline, and untroubled by jarring cries of expostulation often heard in psalms of lament. Faith gives the assurance that Yahweh's faithfulness is a sure defense:

For he will rescue you from the fowler's snare,
 from the fatal plague.
With his pinions he will cover you,
 and under his wings you'll seek refuge.
A shield and rampart is his faithfulness.

Psalm 91:3-4

The speaker goes on to say somewhat effusively that trust in Yahweh protects one from hostile (perhaps demonic) attack (vs. 5-6), from pestilence that strikes people right and left (vs. 7-8), from dangerous experiences (vs. 11-13). The sweeping promise is given that because Yahweh/Elyon is a "safe retreat" (v. 9),

no disaster shall befall you,
no calamity shall come near your tent.

—Psalm 91:10

C.   Divine Oracle (Ps. 91:14-16)
    As indicated by the grammatical shift from third to first person, the final verses are presented as an oracle, Yahweh being the speaker. The effect of the pronouncement is to endorse the trust of *the person* who has been addressed—though not necessarily to confirm all of the simplistic "teaching" given in the preceding part. Notice that the divine approval is given to one who "knows" Yahweh's name (identity); and thus stands in an "I-thou" relationship. (Recall our previous discussion of the name of God, Chapter 5.)

Because he clings to me, I will deliver him,
I will protect him because he knows my name.
When he invokes me [by name], I will answer him.
I will be with him in distress,
I will rescue him and give him honor.
With a long life I will satisfy him,
and let him see my salvation.

—Psalm 91:14-16

The danger of this psalm is that it may encourage a one-sided and immature view of what divine protection means. In too much popular piety, faith in God becomes an insurance against trouble, and prayer becomes a form of magic. It is significant that in the New Testament story of Jesus' temptations in the wilderness, one of Satan's tests is supported by quoting a passage from this psalm, namely, vs. 11-12, which promises that God's angel will "guard you in all your ways" (see Matt. 4:6; Luke 4:10-11). Satan's test was insidious because it was based on a truth, not a falsehood, for God's "faithfulness" is indeed "a shield and a rampart" (v. 4c). But this truth can easily be distorted, even by people of religious faith. It must be read in the larger theological context of Scripture which shows that, in ways past our understanding, God's purpose embraces all the ups and downs of human life and that "in everything God works for good with those who love him" (Rom. 8:28).

MEDITATIONS ON THE GOOD LIFE

In the Psalter we find a number of psalms that reflect the wisdom movement. This movement, as we know increasingly from archaeology and the study of ancient culture, was diffused throughout the whole ancient Near East—Egypt, Canaan, the fringes of Arabia, Asia Minor, Mesopotamia. Very early this movement made its impact on Israel, with the result that Solomon came to be regarded as the patron of wisdom, and important wisdom writings, such as Proverbs and Ecclesiastes, were attributed to him. In Israel, however, the wisdom movement developed a distinctive Israelite accent, as evidenced in the proverb: "The fear of Yahweh is the beginning of wisdom" (Prov. 9:10; Job 28:28; Ps. 111:10). Israel's sages insisted that wisdom does not come just from observing human conduct or through rational reflection on the teachings handed down in the wisdom schools. Rather, the "beginning" (that is, the foundation or the premise) of wisdom is *faith*—faith in Yahweh, the God who is known and worshiped in Israel.

Wisdom motifs found their way into Israelite psalms at an early period. For instance, Psalm 78, one of the storytelling psalms to which we have alluded several times, begins in the style of a wisdom poem (vs. 1-4). In v. 2 the recitation of Yahweh's deeds and the people's unfaithfulness is specifically called a wisdom utterance (Hebrew *mashal*, "parable"). The purpose of the psalm is to edify the congregation through the recollection of a shared history, so that the people may learn from the past how to live in the present. The introduction to this psalm is like the opening of Psalm 49, in which a wisdom meditation upon the transience of life is brought into the context of worship.

Hear this, all peoples!
    Give ear, all inhabitants of the world,
both low and high,
    rich and poor together!
My mouth shall speak wisdom;
    the meditation of my heart shall be understanding.
I will incline my ear to a proverb [mashal];
    I will solve my riddle to the music of the lyre.
                    —Psalm 49:1-4 (RSV)

These psalms show that the Israelite faith did not advocate "a sacrifice of the intellect"—such as is made in some situations today when people "check" their intellects, along with coats and hats, in the vestibule before entering the sanctuary! Rather, wisdom belongs in the context of worship, as attested by the presence of wisdom psalms in the Psalter.

WISDOM PSALMS

36 "With thee is the fountain of life"
[This psalm is a mixed composition, having elements of wisdom (vs. 1-4), hymn (vs. 5-9), and lament (vs. 10-21)]
*37 "The mouth of the righteous utters wisdom"
*49 "My mouth shall speak wisdom"
*73 "Nevertheless I am continually with thee"
[Classification as a wisdom psalm is uncertain]
78 "I will open my mouth in a parable"
[A narrative or storytelling psalm]
112 "Light arises in the darkness for the upright"
[An alphabetical acrostic psalm]
127 "The fruit of the womb a reward"
128 "It shall be well with you"
133 "When brothers dwell in unity"

(See also Prov. 8; Ecclus. 14:20–15:10)

Captions are from the RSV.

There is much difference of opinion about the criteria for determining wisdom psalms and about the number of psalms that should be included in this category. The influence of Israelite sages was so widespread that wisdom motifs were employed in prophetic speech and appeared in various types of psalms (laments, thanksgivings, hymns). Roland Murphy proposes that we should look for the following elements in deciding about the classification of wisdom psalms:[7]

1. A sharp contrast between the righteous and the wicked
2. Advice about conduct that results in either welfare or misfortune
3. The premise that "the fear [reverence] of Yahweh" is the starting point of wisdom
4. Comparisons and admonitions that are used to exhort one to good conduct
5. Alphabetical acrostic pattern
6. "Better than" sayings (cf. Prov. 17:1; 19:1)
7. The address "my son" customary in wisdom schools
8. The approving word "blessed" (happy, fortunate)

Not all these features would have to be found in every psalm to identify it as a wisdom type. However, a number of them are present in Psalms 37 and 49, which are generally agreed to be wisdom psalms.

Wisdom psalms are not immediately and essentially connected with specific acts of worship, and therefore may be considered noncultic. Although they refer to going to the sanctuary (Ps. 73:17) or use the metaphor of finding refuge under Yahweh's wings (Ps. 36:7)—a reference to the wings of the cherubim outstretched over the Ark in the Holy of Holies—they are essentially meditations on the good life. Often they begin with beatitudes ("blessed [happy] is the one who . . .") or contain admonitions against following evil and foolish ways. The ultimate background of this instruction is the ancient doctrine of the Two Ways as taught in wisdom circles: the way of life which the wise pursue and the way of destruction which the foolish follow (cf. Matt. 7:13-14). According to Israel's faith, however, this instruction does not have its source in human wisdom; rather, it is a divine gift. Yahweh teaches people to walk in "the right paths," the paths of salvation. Accordingly, in Israel's wisdom psalms true wisdom is identified with "the fear of Yahweh" and, even more specifically, with faithfulness to Yahweh's torah (teaching, instruction; often weakly translated "law"). One of the stanzas in Psalm 37, which is based on the alphabetical acrostic pattern, says:

The mouth of the righteous utters wisdom,
  and his tongue speaks justice.
The law [torah] of his God is in his heart;
  his steps do not slip.
                —Psalm 37:30-31 (RSV)

Closely related to the wisdom psalms listed above are several psalms that extol the *torah* of Yahweh as the medium through which the will of God is known and hence the basis for true wisdom and happiness.

TORAH PSALMS

✓*1	"Like a tree planted by streams of water"
*19:	
7-14	"More to be desired than gold"
	[The first part of the psalm is a creation hymn]
119	"O how I love thy law!"
	[An alphabetical acrostic psalm]

Captions are from the RSV.

As we have already noticed, our English word "law" is an inadequate translation of the Hebrew word *torah*. This usual translation, which is also found in the New Testament (Greek *nomos*, "law"), suggests an inhibiting legalism ("the bondage of the law") from which persons need to be set free so that they may have life abundantly.

But the knowledge of Yahweh's *torah* is the occasion for the heart to rejoice, as one psalmist says (Ps. 19:8), and this kind of celebration still takes place in the Jewish festival called Simhat Hat-Torah (Rejoicing in the Torah).

The Hebrew word *torah* is rich with meaning. It may refer to the story of Yahweh's actions to create a people and guide them into the future, as in the storytelling psalms (see Chapter 2); or it may refer to the obligations (i.e., precepts, commandments) that shape the life-style of a people who tell and retell the story. These two dimensions—narration and obligation or, in Jewish tradition, *haggadah* and *halakah*—are so inseparable that it is impossible to think of one without thinking of the other. Torah in this twofold sense was mediated to the people through a chain of tradition that went back to Moses, the fountainhead. However, eventually, in the period of the exile and restoration, about the time of Nehemiah and Ezra, the Torah was mediated in written form, as "scripture." The scriptural Torah was identified preeminently with the first five books of the Bible, the Pentateuch.

According to the psalm that introduces the whole Psalter, the wise person is the one who reads and meditates on the Torah day and night. Psalm 1 begins with a beatitude ("Blessed . . .") typical of a wisdom poem, as in Jeremiah 17:5-8, a wisdom utterance that may have influenced the psalmist. In both instances the wise person, who ponders the torah, is likened to "a tree planted by waters" that bears fruit in its proper season in contrast to the foolish (wicked) who are like evanescent chaff, driven away by the wind. The psalm has a symmetrical structure in which contrasting (positive and negative) statements are balanced for the purpose of teaching.

[positive] 1. Blessed are those who do not . . . [negative]
         Rather . . .   [positive]
         Result
[negative] 2. Not so are the wicked . . .
         Rather
         Result
       3. Summary, introduced by "for" *(ki)*

Fortunate are those who
do not follow the counsel of the wicked
do not stand in the way [life-style] of sinners,
and do not sit in the company of the insolent.

Rather, in the Torah of Yahweh they delight,
and on his Torah they ponder day and night.

They are like a tree planted by a fresh stream,
that yields its fruit at the proper time,
and whose foliage never fades.
Whatever they do comes to fruition!

Not so are the wicked, not so.
Rather, they are like chaff the wind scatters.

Hence, in the divine judgment the wicked will not stand,
nor sinners [stand] in the community of the righteous.

For *[ki]* Yahweh recognizes the way of the righteous,
but the way of the wicked leads to naught.
—Psalm 1:1-6

Some may regard this as an "achievement" psalm: the
wise person who lives by the torah is successful, while the
one who flouts it is a failure. But this simplistic view
hardly does justice to the poem. Here the psalmist sharply
contrasts two attitudes—or, as we would say today, two
life-styles. On the one hand, there are the persons who
humbly acknowledge their dependence on God and seek
to know God's will by studying the Torah. They live by a

personal relationship to God, striving constantly, and listening intently, for the word of God day and night. They may not be great persons, as the world measures greatness, but they are blessed by a serene sense of the God-given meaning of life. On the other hand, there are persons who care nothing about the religious tradition, who are determined to live out of their own resources, and who are scornful of the devout life. Such persons belong in the category of the "fool" who says in his heart (mind), "There is no God" (Ps. 10:4; 14:1), that is, the practical atheist who supposes that a person can live as he or she pleases and get away with it because God is not to be taken seriously. These people, says the psalmist, are like the chaff that the wind blows away during a threshing of the wheat, for their existence lacks deep rootage.

The theme of seeking to know the will of God, which is developed with chaste simplicity in Psalm 1, is expanded to almost wearisome length in Psalm 119, the longest psalm in the Psalter. Various passages in this psalm show that it is a struggle to know and do God's will, a struggle that is waged in the face of adverse experiences and threats to one's existence (e.g., Ps. 119:153-160).

The only unity that this long psalm has is provided by the Hebrew alphabet: each successive stanza begins with the next letter of the alphabet. The first eight-line stanza begins with the first letter (aleph), the second eight lines with the second letter (beth), and so on through the twenty-two letters of the alphabet. This acrostic scheme was a convenient device for use in teaching or memorizing, but psalms of this kind seem to be far removed from poems that were actually shaped by liturgical usage or even those which imitated cultic forms. Two of the psalms listed above as wisdom psalms are alphabetical acrostics (Ps. 37 and 112), and this pattern is followed in other types of psalms.

ALPHABETICAL ACROSTIC PSALMS

Psalms 9-10	Individual lament
Psalm 25	Individual lament
Psalm 34	Individual song of thanksgiving
Psalm 37	Wisdom psalm
Psalm 111	Hymn
Psalm 112	Wisdom psalm
Psalm 119	Torah psalm
Psalm 145	Hymn

THE ENIGMAS OF LIFE

Wisdom and torah psalms agree on one premise: actions have consequences. The person whose life-style is based on the fear of Yahweh and the teachings of the Torah is "happy" (fortunate); the person whose actions and attitudes have another foundation is denied this felicity. At first consideration it seems that this is a pragmatic philosophy, one that measures the truth of religious beliefs by their practical results. Admittedly, many people then, as now, were tempted by a simplistic view of the blessings that result from faith in God or the curses that may fall upon the disbeliever. At their depth, however, the biblical psalms do not express an easygoing pragmatism but rest upon a theology of creation. The action-consequence pattern is written into the very fabric of the universe that was created and ordered by God. Those who are wise strive to attune their actions to the cosmic order; those who are foolish violate this order and bring upon themselves the inevitable consequences. Israel's sages would have agreed with the statement of Paul that God is not to be mocked, "for whatever one sows, that will one reap" (Gal. 6:7).

In some wisdom circles, represented, for instance, by the book of Ecclesiastes, sages become pessimistic about the ability of human wisdom to penetrate the divine "secret" of the creation and to know the will of the Creator. However, the wisdom psalms of the Psalter are more optimistic, and the main reason for this is their conviction that God has revealed in the Torah the precepts that enable one to live in harmony with the Creator's will. Psalm 19, which we considered earlier (Chapter 5), shows the correspondence between the marvelous order of the cosmos (Psalm 19A) and the ordering will of God revealed through the Torah (Psalm 19B).

Hence these psalms give the assurance that those who fear Yahweh and obey the divine teaching *(torah)* will enjoy the good life—not in another world, but in this historical world, here and now. A faithful relationship with God will mean the enjoyment of God and, consequently, the tasting of life's goodness. Such a person will experience all that "salvation" involves: health, wholeness, welfare, the freedom to be, and to serve God, in the covenant community.

It is this healthy, life-affirming attitude, however, which prompts the question with which these wisdom psalms wrestle: why is it that things often work out so badly for the God-fearing person and so well for the one who is careless about, or defiant of, God? Three wisdom psalms, Psalms 37, 49, and 73, are especially concerned with this problem—one that has plagued people of faith down through the centuries. Beyond the Psalter, The Book of Job is preeminently addressed to this problem.[8]

The simple solution to the problem—the one advanced by friends of Job—was to say that life's imbalances are only temporary and will be rectified shortly. In the meantime, suffering is, at best, the chastening or correction of the Almighty (Job 5:17-27). Yet one has only to read Psalm 37 to realize that this kind of answer is a whistling in the dark. Here the psalmist goes all the way with the doctrine: just be patient and you will see the reward of the righteous and the retribution of the wicked. Indeed, at one point he blandly testifies:

I have been young, and now am old;
yet I have not seen the righteous forsaken
or his children begging bread.
—Psalm 37:25 (RSV)

The appropriate response to this statement is that the psalmist either had not lived long enough, or that he must have lived someplace where he was sheltered from the hard realities of life! Furthermore, the possibility has to be reckoned with—as at the end of The Book of Job—that suffering *may* be the occasion for a deeper understanding of one's relationship to God.

Psalm 73, the greatest of the wisdom psalms, grapples with this problem at the profoundest level in the whole Psalter, and in so doing comes closest to the testimony of Job. The psalmist begins by asserting the "orthodox" thesis:

Truly God is good to the upright,
to those who are pure in heart.
—Psalm 73:1 (RSV)

Then follows the crucial "but" (v. 2)—the adversative conjunction—which was dictated by the psalmist's own experience. When he considered the imbalances of life, so we read, his faith was almost destroyed (vs. 2-16). The only thing that restrained him from speaking out his doubts was his concern for the effect that it would have on the younger generation!

Searching for an answer to this baffling problem was a "wearisome task," and the psalmist confesses that he was about to surrender his faith:

Until I went into the sanctuary of God;
then I perceived their end.
Truly thou dost set them in slippery places;
thou dost make them fall to ruin.
How they are destroyed in a moment,
swept away utterly by terrors!
They are like a dream when one awakes,
on awaking you despise their phantoms.
—Psalm 73:17-20 (RSV)

Like Job, the psalmist was ready to recant his presumptuous attempt to judge the ways of God from the limited standpoint of his experience (cf. Job 42:1-6). But, like Job, he too seemed to break through the limitations of his past understanding into a new apprehension of God's presence and power, which his theology, however orthodox, could not fully comprehend. The turning point in the psalm is indicated by another adversative conjunction—"the great nevertheless" which stands at the beginning of v. 23:

Nevertheless I am continually with thee;
thou dost hold my right hand.
Thou dost guide me with thy counsel,
and afterward thou wilt receive me to glory.
—Psalm 73:23-24 (RSV)

The meaning of the last sentence, unfortunately, is obscure in the Hebrew. It may be, as some interpreters have insisted, one of the few places in the Old Testament where there is an "intimation of immortality," that is, a hope for a breakthrough into a new form of existence in which, as Paul put it, "the mortal puts on immortality" in a mystery which is comprehended solely in God's grace (I Cor. 15:42-58). But if it is an intimation, it is no more. The psalmist is not really concerned with what lies beyond the boundary of death, but with the solution to existential problems which *now* demand an answer if one is to live in faith—and die in faith. A similar view, it seems, is expressed at one point in another wisdom psalm:

> This is the fate of those who have foolish confidence,
> the end of those who are pleased with their portion.
> Like sheep they are appointed for Sheol;
> Death shall be their shepherd;
> straight to the grave they descend,
> and their form shall waste away;
> Sheol shall be their home.
> But God will ransom my soul [*nefesh,* "being"]
> from the power of Sheol,
> for he will receive me.
> —Psalm 49:13-15 (RSV)

Psalm 73 speaks for us in our time—not because it gives a theological answer, but because it portrays the situation in which new theological formulations must be found. Today we know, even more radically than the wisdom psalmist, that theological formulations which were satisfactory in a previous day no longer cope with the hard realities of contemporary human experience. How can one talk about the "happiness" of the God-fearing in a world where six million Jews were burned in Nazi ovens, where many people are doomed to live out their lives in economic ghettos, where the threat of atomic annihilation hangs over every military adventure, where science is pushing back our historical horizons into the vast reaches of the cosmos? Theology that is vital stands on the boundary between the old theology which has been systematized and the new theology which must be formulated. And if a person's intellect is to be brought into the sanctuary of God, this standing on the boundary between the old and the new is imperative.[9]

It is appropriate to conclude this discussion with the well-known Psalm 90 which, though technically not a wisdom psalm, was profoundly influenced by the wisdom movement. In structure, this psalm is a community lament occasioned by a situation of sore distress that threatens human welfare and security.

A. Address to God (Psalm 90:1-6)
   The first part (vs. 1-6) opens with an address to Yahweh, who existed before the creation and whose sovereignty transcends all the boundaries of time. Strikingly, here at the beginning, as well as at the end (v. 17), Yahweh is addressed as Adonai (Lord), a title of majesty (cf. Ps. 8:1).

Lord, you have been
  our refuge age after age.
Before the mountains were born,
  before the earth or the world came to birth,
  you were God from all eternity and for ever.
                    —Psalm 90:1-2 (JB)

   In hymnic fashion this address is expanded in two "thou" strophes that ascribe praise to the almighty Sovereign, each of which contrasts human transience with God's eternity (vs. 3-4 and 5-6).

B. Lament in Distress (Psalm 90:7-10)
   After the address to God comes a twofold description of human distress, a description that transcends any situation of Israel's lament and speaks to the human condition generally.

   First, human life is lived under the judgment (wrath) of God, from whose penetrating scrutiny there is no escape even in the innermost secrets of one's life (vs. 7-8)—a theme that is developed exquisitely in Psalm 139.

Secondly, the wise person is the one who knows the limitations and transience of human life and acts accordingly in sober faith.

> Our days dwindle under your wrath,
>   our lives are over in a breath
>   —our life lasts for seventy years,
>   eighty with good health.
> But they all add up to anxiety and trouble—
>   over in a trice, and then we are gone.
>
>   —Psalm 90:9-10 (JB)

This movement of the psalm concludes with a prayer that God will bestow the gift of wisdom which recognizes human fallibility and mortality.

> Teach us to count how few days we have,
>   and so gain wisdom of heart.
>   —Psalm 90:12 (JB)

C. Prayer for Help (Psalm 90:13-17)
The final movement of the psalm, consistent with the lament form (see pp. 75-77), is a petition introduced by the typical cry of lament, "How long?" (e.g., Ps. 13:1-3). Speaking for the community of faith, the psalmist prays that we may awake in the morning (cf. Ps. 139:18) filled with confidence in Yahweh's *hesed*, or covenant loyalty. Human trust is grounded in the God who, as announced at the opening of the psalm, transcends all times, whose sovereignty is "from everlasting to everlasting." Because our transient lives, from beginning to end, are embraced within

the Creator's faithfulness, says the psalmist, we may rejoice all of our hastening days and may live, and die, in the confidence that "the work of our hands" will be conserved and glorified in God's eternal purpose.

HUMAN GRANDEUR AND MISERY

A rabbi observed that a person should carry in a pocket two stones, one inscribed with "For my sake the world was created," and the other with "I am but dust and ashes." And each stone should be pulled out, as the occasion requires, to remind us of who we are in God's creation.

This is a good illustration of the "wisdom" that is found in the psalms. There are psalms, as we have seen earlier (see the discussion of Ps. 8, pp. 151-154), which exalt human beings to a position of supremacy in God's creation and which endow them with the role of expressing the praise of the whole creation to the Creator. Human beings are called to be kings and queens in God's earthly estate. Though related to the *'adamah* ("soil"), like the animals, as portrayed in the paradise story (Gen. 2-3), human beings transcend the natural world and are objects of God's concern. The tremendous achievements in the fields of medicine, transportation, communication, space exploration, music and the arts—to mention only a few—may be regarded as the exercise of the task that God has given to human beings to be agents of the divine rule that governs the cosmos. Against philosophies that reduce the human to the level of nature, Israel's psalmists enable one to say: "For my sake the world was created."

On the other hand, the high position of human beings in God's cosmic administration may tempt them to live like the "fool" who says, "There is no God" (Ps. 10:4; 14:1). When human beings attempt to "play God," as though they were running the show, their royal dominion over the earth leads to the picture portrayed in the primeval history (Gen. 2-11): violence that corrupts the earth, to the point that chaos is about to return. Wisdom psalms humble us with the sober reminder that human life, in contrast to God's eternity, is evanescent, like the flash of a firefly in the night. Frail and earthly creatures we are, made from the dust and returning to the dust.

> You turn humanity back into dust;
> "Turn back," you say, "human beings!"
> —Psalm 90:3

In the wisdom perspective of Psalm 90, all our vaunted achievements, impressive as they are, mean nothing except for God's faithfulness (ḥesed) which overarches and undergirds human life from birth to death. So, when we are tempted to think of ourselves more highly than we ought to think, Israel's sages teach us to say, "I am but dust and ashes."

READING THE PSALMS IN THE CHRIST CONTEXT

We return, then, to the question that was raised at the outset of this study: In what sense does the Psalter speak to us of Jesus Christ? The New Testament wrestles with this question in various passages by saying that the psalms not only anticipate the advent of the King who would inaugurate God's kingdom but portray the passion and struggle he would undergo in fulfilling his task. Today we can say with greater clarity that the whole history of Israel, from the oppression in Egypt and on, was a passion story in which Israel experienced the reality of God in the midst of suffering, a suffering which—as the prophet Second Isaiah perceived—was borne vicariously in order that the nations and the whole creation might rejoice in the God who is Creator and Lord. The psalms show, as Christoph Barth observes, that "Jesus and Israel belong together, and that their respective histories cannot be understood apart from each other."[10] From the Christian point of view the story of Jesus and the story of Israel constitute *one* story: the story in which God is involved personally and redemptively in the historical experiences of a people to open a way into the future in which all peoples ultimately may find true peace (welfare).

Psalm 73, as we have noticed, reaches a turning point in "the great nevertheless." This is not an adversative which turns us away from the problems of existence; rather, it turns us toward the world with the confidence that God is present and at work there. In its simplest terms this faith affirms, "Nevertheless, I am continually with thee." On a profounder level this Biblical faith joyfully announces that, because of God's victory in Jesus Christ, "in all these things we are more than conquerors through him who loved us":

> *For I am sure that neither death, nor life, nor angels, nor principalities, nor things present, nor things to come, nor powers, nor height, nor depth, nor anything else in all creation, will be able to separate us from the love of God in Christ Jesus our Lord.*
>
> *—Romans 8:38-39 (RSV)*

Such a confession, which is ever open to new theological formulations, is an invitation to join with the community of faith in the singing of the laments, the songs of thanksgiving, and the hymns of the Psalter in the name of Christ and to the glory of God.

NOTES

1. Aage Bentzen, *Introduction to the Old Testament*, Vol. 2, 4th ed. (Copenhagen: G. E. C. Gads Forlag, 1958), p. 170. Bentzen observes: "The Book of Psalms is not only a ritual song book, but also, and perhaps more, a 'Wisdom Book,' a book showing the way of a righteous life."

2. Also Ps. 13:5; 52:8; 73:23; 141:8. This "adversative conjunction" is discussed by Claus Westermann, *The Praise of God in the Psalms*, 2d ed., trans. Keith R. Crim (John Knox Press, 1965), pp. 70-75.

3. Comment on Ps. 27:4 by Artur Weiser, *The Psalms, A Commentary*, trans. Herbert Hartwell, The Old Testament Library (Westminster Press, 1962), p. 248.

4. This interpretation is influenced by John Paterson's exposition of Psalm 23 in *The Praises of Israel* (Charles Scribner's Sons, 1950), pp. 108-115, which, in turn, depends upon a study by George Adam Smith.

5. Weiser, *The Psalms, A Commentary*, p. 227.

6. This is the view of Hans-Joachim Kraus, *Psalmen*, Vol. 2, Biblischer Kommentar: Altes Testament (Neukirchen-Vluyn: Neukirchener Verlag, 1960), pp. 635-640, who draws attention to the parallel in Psalm 34, where a person in a situation of thanksgiving teaches others out of personal experience.

7. Roland E. Murphy, *The Psalms, Job*, Proclamation Commentaries (Fortress Press, 1977). See also "Psalms," in *The Jerome Biblical Commentary* (Prentice-Hall, 1969), pp. 569-602.

8. See the discussion of Israel's Wisdom literature, including The Book of Job, in Bernhard W. Anderson, *Understanding the Old Testament*, 3d ed. (Prentice-Hall, 1975), Ch. 17.

9. See the illuminating essay by Martin Buber, "The Heart Determines: Psalm 73," in *Theodicy in the Old Testament*, ed. James L. Crenshaw (Fortress Press, 1983), pp. 109-118.

10. Christoph Barth, *Introduction to the Psalms*, trans. R. A. Wilson (Charles Scribner's Sons, 1966), p. 70.

APPENDIX A
Outline of Psalms
Considered in This Study

(Asterisks mark psalms recommended for special reading.
Some psalms are listed in more than one place.)

Chapter 2: Narrative or Storytelling Psalms

*78	135
*105	*136
106	

Chapter 3: Laments

COMMUNITY LAMENTS

*12	89:38-51 (royal lament)
*44	*90
58	*94
60	123
74	126
79	129
*80	137
83	Lamentations 5
*85	

INDIVIDUAL LAMENTS

*3	27:7-14
*4 (song of trust?)	28
5	*31
7	35
9-10	36
*13	*39
14 (= 53)	40:12-17
17	41
*22	*42-43
25	52
26	53 (= 14)

54	*77
55	86
56	*88
*57	89:38-51 (royal lament)
59	109
61	120
63	*139
64	140
*69	141
70 (= 40:13-17)	142
*71	Lamentations 3

PENITENTIAL PSALMS

*6	*102
*32 (song of thanksgiving)	*130
*38	*143
*51	

Chapter 4: Songs of Thanksgiving

COMMUNITY SONGS OF THANKSGIVING

65 (hymn?)	*124
67 (hymn?)	136 (hymn?)
75	I Samuel 2:1-10
*107	

INDIVIDUAL SONGS OF THANKSGIVING

18 (= II Sam. 22)	*92
(royal thanksgiving)	*103 (probably a hymn)
21 (royal thanksgiving)	108 (= 57:5-11; 60:5-12)
30	*116
*32 (penitential psalm)	*118 (royal thanksgiving)
*34	*138
40:1-11	Isaiah 38:9-20
66:13-20	Jonah 2:2-9

Chapter 5: Hymns of Praise

I. HYMNS TO GOD, WHO CREATED (REDEEMED) ISRAEL

66:1-12	149
*100	*Exodus 15:1-18
111	Deuteronomy 32:1-43
*114	Habakkuk 3:2-19
	Isaiah 52:7-10

II. HYMNS TO GOD, WHO CREATED THE WORLD
("CREATION PSALMS")

*8	*104
*19:1-6	*148
95:1-7a	See also: 74:12-17, 89:5-18

III. HYMNS TO THE CREATOR AND RULER OF HISTORY

*33	*145
*103 (song of thanksgiving?)	*146
113	*147
117	150 (doxology)

See also "Enthronement Psalms" and "Songs of Zion," Chapter 6)

Chapter 6: Festival Songs and Liturgies

COVENANT RENEWAL LITURGIES

50	*81

ENTHRONEMENT PSALMS

24 (entrance liturgy)	*96
29	97
*47	*98
93	*99
*95	

PSALMS OF THE DAVIDIC COVENANT

*78 (storytelling psalm)	*89 (royal hymn and lament)
	*132

ROYAL PSALMS

*2	72
*18 (royal thanksgiving)	101
20	*110
21	144:1-11 (royal lament)
45	

SONGS OF ZION

*46	
48	87
76	*121
*84	*122

LITURGIES

15 (compare Ps. 24)	115
68	134
82	

Chapter 7: Songs of Trust and Meditation

SONGS OF TRUST

11	63 (individual lament?)
16	*91
*23	*121
*27:1-6	125 (community lament?)
62	131

WISDOM PSALMS

36 (mixed type)	127
*37	128
*49	133
*73	Proverbs 8
78 (storytelling psalm)	Ecclesiasticus 14:20–15:10
112	

TORAH PSALMS

*1	
*19:7-14	119

APPENDIX B

Index of Psalms According to Type

The following is presented only as a working basis for the study of the Psalms. There are too many uncertainties to permit an exact and rigid classification according to type.

Psalm	Type
BOOK I	
1	Torah (wisdom) psalm
2	Royal psalm
3	Individual lament
4	Individual lament (psalm of trust?)
5	Individual lament
6	Individual lament (penitential psalm)
7	Individual lament
8	Hymn
9-10	Individual lament? (alphabetical acrostic)
11	Song of trust
12	Community lament
13	Individual lament
14	(= 53) Individual lament
15	Liturgy for admission to the cult
16	Song of trust
17	Individual lament
18	(= II Sam. 22) Individual thanksgiving (royal)
19:1-6	Hymn
19:7-14	Torah (wisdom) psalm
20	Royal psalm
21	Royal psalm (thanksgiving)
22	Individual lament
23	Song of trust
24	Temple entrance liturgy
25	Individual lament (alphabetical acrostic)
26	Individual lament
27:1-6	Song of trust
27:7-14	Individual lament
28	Individual lament
29	Hymn
30	Individual song of thanksgiving

Psalm	Type
31	Individual lament
32	Individual song of thanksgiving (penitential psalm with wisdom elements)
33	Hymn
34	Individual song of thanksgiving (alphabetical acrostic with wisdom elements)
35	Individual lament
36	(Mixed type, including wisdom, hymn, lament)
37	Wisdom psalm (alphabetical acrostic)
38	Individual lament (penitential psalm)
39	Individual lament
40:1-11	Individual song of thanksgiving
40:12-17	Individual lament
41	Individual lament

BOOK II

Psalm	Type
42-43	Individual lament
44	Community lament
45	Royal psalm
46	Hymn: Song of Zion
47	Hymn (Enthronement psalm)
48	Hymn: Song of Zion
49	Wisdom psalm
50	Covenant renewal liturgy
51	Individual lament (penitential psalm)
52	Individual lament (mixture of types)
53	(= 14) Individual lament
54	Individual lament
55	Individual lament
56	Individual lament
57	Individual lament
58	Community lament
59	Individual lament
60	Community lament
61	Individual lament
62	Song of trust
63	Song of trust (or individual lament)
64	Individual lament
65	Community song of thanksgiving (hymn?)
66:1-12	Hymn
66:13-20	Individual song of thanksgiving
67	Community song of thanksgiving (hymn?)
68	Zion liturgy (?) [Almost impossible to classify]
69	Individual lament
70	(= 40:13-17) Individual lament
71	Individual lament
72	Royal psalm

Psalm	Type
BOOK III	
73	Wisdom psalm
74	Community lament
75	Community song of thanksgiving (?)
76	Hymn: Song of Zion
77	Individual lament
78	Storytelling psalm based on the Davidic covenant
79	Community lament
80	Community lament
81	Covenant renewal liturgy
82	Liturgy
83	Community lament
84	Hymn: Song of Zion
85	Community lament
86	Individual lament
87	Hymn: Song of Zion
88	Individual lament
89	Royal psalm based on the Davidic covenant
	89:1-37 Hymn
	89:38-51 Lament

BOOK IV	
90	Community lament
91	Song of trust (including an oracle of protection)
92	Individual song of thanksgiving
93	Hymn (Enthronement psalm)
94	Community lament
95	Hymn ⎫
96	Hymn ⎪
97	Hymn ⎬ Enthronement psalms
98	Hymn ⎪
99	Hymn ⎭
100	Hymn
101	Royal psalm
102	Individual lament including hymnic elements (penitential)
103	Hymn
104	Hymn
105	Storytelling psalm (in mood of hymnic praise)
106	Storytelling psalm (in penitential mood)

BOOK V	
107	Community song of thanksgiving
108	(= 57:7-11; 60:5-12) Mixed type
109	Individual lament
110	Royal psalm
111	Hymn (alphabetical acrostic)

241   *Appendixes*

Psalm	Type
112	Wisdom psalm (alphabetical acrostic)
113	Hymn
114	Hymn
115	Liturgy
116	Individual song of thanksgiving
117	Hymn
118	Individual song of thanksgiving (royal)
119	Torah (wisdom) psalm (alphabetical acrostic)
120	Individual lament
121	Song of trust
122	Song of Zion
123	Community lament
124	Community song of thanksgiving
125	Song of trust (community lament?)
126	Community lament (?)
127	Wisdom psalm
128	Wisdom psalm
129	Community lament (?)
130	Individual lament (penitential psalm)
131	Song of trust
132	Royal psalm: Liturgy of the Davidic covenant
133	Wisdom psalm
134	Liturgy
135	Storytelling psalm: hymnic praise
136	Storytelling psalm: hymnic praise
137	Community lament
138	Individual song of thanksgiving
139	Individual lament (wisdom psalm?)
140	Individual lament
141	Individual lament
142	Individual lament
143	Individual lament
144:1-11	Royal psalm
145	Hymn (alphabetical acrostic)
146	Hymn
147	Hymn
148	Hymn
149	Hymn
150	Hymn: Doxology to conclude the Psalter

APPENDIX C

Quotations from Old Testament Psalms in the New Testament

Echoes of Old Testament psalms are heard in more New Testament passages than those included in this list, which is confined for the most part to direct quotations or specific allusions.

Old Testament Psalm	New Testament Context
Ex. 15:1-18	Rev. 15:3
Deut. 32:35-36	Rom. 12:19; Heb. 10:30
Ps. 2:1-2	Acts 4:25-26
2:1, 5	Rev. 11:18
2:7	Acts 13:33; Heb. 1:5; 5:5
2:8-9	Rev. 2:26-27; 12:5; 19:15
Ps. 4:4	Eph. 4:26
Ps. 5:9	Rom. 3:13
Ps. 6:8	Mt. 7:23; Lk. 13:27
Ps. 8:2	Mt. 21:16
8:4-6	Heb. 2:6-8
8:6	I Cor. 15:27; Eph. 1:22
Ps. 10:7	Rom. 3:14
Ps. 14:1-3	Rom. 3:10-12
Ps. 16:8-11	Acts 2:25-28, 31
16:10	Acts 2:31; 13:35
Ps. 18:49	Rom. 15:9
19:4	Rom. 10:18
19:9	Rev. 16:7; 19:2
Ps. 22:1	Mt. 27:46; Mk. 15:34
22:7-8	Mt. 27:39; Mk. 15:29; Lk. 23:35
22:8	Mt. 27:43
22:13	I Pet. 5:8
22:16; cf. 69:21	Jn. 19:28
22:18	Mt. 27:35; Mk. 15:24; Lk. 23:34; Jn. 19:24
22:21	II Tim. 4:17
22:22	Heb. 2:12, 17
Ps. 23:1-2	Rev. 7:17
Ps. 24:1; cf. 50:12	I Cor. 10:26
Ps. 31:5	Lk. 23:46
Ps. 32:1-2	Rom. 4:7-8

Old Testament Psalm	New Testament Context
Ps. 33:3, etc. ("new song")	Rev. 5:9; 14:3
Ps. 34:8	I Pet. 2:3
34:12-16	I Pet. 3:10-12
34:20	Jn. 19:36
Ps. 35:19	Jn. 15:25
Ps. 36:1	Rom. 3:18
Ps. 37:11	Mt. 5:5
Ps. 40:6-8	Heb. 10:5-7, 8-10
Ps. 41:9	Jn. 13:18
Ps. 42:6, 12; 43:5	Mt. 26:38; Mk. 14:34
Ps. 44:22	Rom. 8:36
Ps. 45:6-7	Heb. 1:8-9
Ps. 48:2	Mt. 5:35
Ps. 50:12; cf. 24:1	I Cor. 10:26
50:14, 23	Mt. 5:33; Heb. 13:15
Ps. 51:4	Rom. 3:4
Ps. 53:1-2	Rom. 3:10-12
Ps. 55:22	I Pet. 5:7
Ps. 68:18	Eph. 4:8
Ps. 69:4	Jn. 15:25
69:9	Jn. 2:17; Rom. 15:3
69:21	Mt. 27:34, 48; Mk. 15:36; Lk. 23:36; Jn. 19:28
69:22-23	Rom. 11:9-10
69:25	Acts 1:20
69:28	Rev. 3:5; 17:8; 20:12; 21:27
Ps. 75:8	Rev. 14:10
Ps. 78:2	Mt. 13:35
78:24; cf. 105:40	Jn. 6:31
Ps. 82:6	Jn. 10:34
Ps. 86:8-10	Rev. 3:9; 15:4
Ps. 89:3-4	Acts 2:30
89:26-27; cf. II Sam. 7:14	Heb. 1:5b
89:27	Rev. 1:5
Ps. 90:4	II Pet. 3:8
Ps. 91:11-12	Mt. 4:6; Lk. 4:10-11
91:13	Lk. 10:19
Ps. 94:11	I Cor. 3:20
94:14	cf. Rom. 11:1-2
Ps. 95:7-8	Heb. 4:7
95:7-11	Heb. 3:7-11
95:11	Heb. 4:3
Ps. 97:7	Heb. 1:6
Ps. 102:25-27	Heb. 1:10-12
Ps. 103:8; cf. 111:4	Jas. 5:11

Old Testament Psalm	New Testament Context
Ps. 104:4	Heb. 1:7
Ps. 105:40; cf. 78:24	Jn. 6:31
Ps. 106:20	cf. Rom. 1:23
Ps. 109:8	Acts 1:20
109:25	Mt. 27:39; Mk. 15:29
Ps. 110:1	Mt. 22:44; 26:64; Mk. 12:36; 14:62; 16:19; Lk. 20:42-43; 22:69; Acts 2:34-35; I Cor. 15:25; Eph. 1:20; Col. 3:1; Heb. 1:13; 8:1; 10:12-13; 12:2
110:4	Heb. 5:6; 7:17; 7:21
Ps. 112:9	II Cor. 9:9
Ps. 115:4-7	Rev. 9:20
115:13	Rev. 11:18; 19:5
Ps. 116:10	II Cor. 4:13
Ps. 117:1	Rom. 15:11
Ps. 118:6	Heb. 13:6
118:22-23	Mt. 21:42; Mk. 12:10; Lk. 20:17; Acts 4:11; I Pet. 2:7
118:25-26	Mt. 21:9, 15; Mk. 11:9-10; Jn. 12:13
118:26	Mt. 23:39; Lk. 13:35; 19:38
Ps. 132:5	Acts 7:46
132:11	Acts 2:30
Ps. 135:15-17	Rev. 9:20
Ps. 137:8	Rev. 18:6
137:9	Lk. 19:44
Ps. 140:3	Rom. 3:13
Ps. 143:2	Rom. 3:20; Gal. 2:16
Ps. 146:6	Acts 2:24; 14:15; Rev. 10:6

SELECTED BIBLIOGRAPHY

Commentaries on the Psalms

Anderson, Arnold A. *The Psalms*. 2 vols. New Century Bible. London: Oliphants, 1972.

Eaton, John H. *Psalms: Introduction and Commentary*. Torch Bible Commentaries. London: SCM Press, 1967.

Kidner, Derek. *The Psalms*. 2 vols. Tyndale Old Testament Commentaries. London: Inter-Varsity Press, 1973, 1975.

Kraus, Hans-Joachim. *Psalmen*. Biblischer Kommentar: Altes Testament. Neukirchen-Vluyn: Neukirchener Verlag, 1960.

Murphy, Roland E. "Psalms," in *The Jerome Biblical Commentary*. Prentice-Hall, 1969.

Rogerson, J. W., and McKay, J. W., eds. *The Psalms*. 3 vols. Cambridge Bible Commentary, based on the NEB. Cambridge University Press, 1977.

Weiser, Artur. *The Psalms, A Commentary*, trans. Herbert Hartwell. The Old Testament Library. Westminster Press, 1962.

General Writings on the Psalms

Ackroyd, Peter R. *Doors of Perception: A Guide to Reading the Psalms*. London: SCM Press, 1978.

Barth, Christoph. *Introduction to the Psalms*, trans. R. A. Wilson. Charles Scribner's Sons, 1966.

Bonhoeffer, Dietrich. *Psalms: The Prayer Book of the Bible*, trans. J. A. Burtness. Augsburg Publishing House, 1970.

Brueggemann, Walter. "From Hurt to Joy, From Death to Life," *Interpretation*, Vol. 28 (1974), pp. 3-19.

Eaton, John H. *Kingship and the Psalms*. London: SCM Press, 1976.

Lewis, C. S. *Reflections on the Psalms*. London: William Collins Sons & Co., 1960.

Miller, Patrick D., Jr., "Trouble and Woe: Interpreting the Biblical Laments," *Interpretation*, Vol. 37 (1983), pp. 32-45.

Murphy, Roland E. "The Faith of the Psalmist," *Interpretation*, Vol. 34 (1980), pp. 229-239.

————. *The Psalms, Job*. Proclamation Commentaries. Fortress Press, 1977.

Ringgren, Helmer. *The Faith of the Psalmists*. Fortress Press, 1963.

Terrien, Samuel. *The Psalms and Their Meaning for Today*. Bobbs-Merrill Co., 1952.

Westermann, Claus. *The Praise of God in the Psalms*, trans. Keith R. Crim. 2d ed. John Knox Press, 1965.

————. "The Role of the Lament in the Theology of the Old Testament," *Interpretation*, Vol. 28 (1974), pp. 20-38.

Special Studies on the Psalms and Worship

Anderson, Bernhard W. *Creation Versus Chaos*. Association Press, 1967. See esp. Ch. 3, "Creation and Worship."

Clements, Ronald E. *God and Temple*. Fortress Press, 1965.

Kraus, Hans-Joachim. *Worship in Israel: A Cultic History of the Old Testament*, trans. Geoffrey Buswell. Rev. and enlarged ed. John Knox Press, 1966.

Shepherd, Massey H. *The Psalms in Christian Worship*. Augsburg Publishing House, 1976.

Werner, Eric. *The Sacred Bridge: The Interdependence of Liturgy and Music in Synagogue and Church During the First Millennium*. Columbia University Press, 1959.

INDEX OF BIBLICAL PASSAGES